COLOR ATLAS
of
FORENSIC
PATHOLOGY

COLOR ATLAS
of
FORENSIC
PATHOLOGY

by Jay Dix

CRC Press
Boca Raton   London   New York   Washington, D.C.

Library of Congress Cataloging-in-Publication Data

Catalog record is available from the Library of Congress.

PREFACE

This atlas is intended for those individuals involved in investigating causes of injury and death. The user does not have to be a physician or pathologist to benefit from this text. In fact, this atlas was not put together specifically for that audience. The intent is to show different causes of injury with case examples for the investigator who can use additional "visuals" in understanding the work they perform. This is not to say that pathologists will not see different types of cases or injuries than in their previous experiences. I am constantly amazed how often I see or hear about something I have not encountered before. I do not believe anyone will ever see it all. That is what makes this field so interesting and exciting.

No atlas can be completely comprehensive and include everything in a particular field. This one is no exception. I believe it does contain much of the basic information which forensic pathologists deal with on a day-to-day basis. The reader will hopefully gain some insight in the many different types of causes of deaths we deal with and how the manners (accident, homicide, suicide, and natural) of death are diagnosed. If the reader understands the information in this text and thinks it can be helpful, then I feel I have been successful.

J.D.

CONTENTS

Chapter I

TIME OF DEATH AND DECOMPOSITION

TIME OF DEATH (POSTMORTEM INTERVAL)

The determination of time of death, or the interval between the time of death and when the body is found (i.e., postmortem interval), can only be *estimated*. Unless there is a witness, the time of someone's death cannot be determined with certainty. The longer the time since death, the greater the chance for error in determining the postmortem interval. There are numerous individual observations which, when used together, provide the best estimate of the time of death. The examiner must check the following: rigor mortis, livor mortis, body temperature, and decompositional changes. A thorough scene investigation is absolutely essential. The physical findings of the body must be compared to witness accounts of when the decedent was last seen or heard. The environment is the single most important factor in determining the postmortem interval because decompositional changes occur much more rapidly in warmer temperatures.

The type of clothing may help indicate what the person was doing and the time of day when death occurred.

The use of gastric contents helps to determine the type of food last eaten. It is not very helpful in determining time of death because of the variability in how a person's system deals with different amounts and types of food.

DETERMINING TIME OF DEATH BY SCENE INVESTIGATION

Clues about the time of death may also be found at the scene away from, near to, or on the body. Evidence such as the type of insects on the body, flora beneath the body, or objects from the decedent's residence may be contributing clues.

Insect larvae on the body can be collected and saved in alcohol. An entomologist will be able to state not only the type of larvae, but also their developmental stage. Each stage has a specific time duration which enables an entomologist to state how long the larvae have been present. It should be remembered, however, that this time estimate is only the time larvae were present on the body.

Flora discovered under or near the body may be helpful. A botanist may be able to examine the specimen, classify the type of flora and time of year it would normally be present, and determine how much time elapsed to reach that particular growth stage.

Information from the scene, other than that associated with the body, may also be critical in estimating the time of death. All clues from a house or an apartment must be analyzed. Was the mail picked up? Were the lights on or off? Was food being prepared? Answering questions such as these may be helpful.

DECOMPOSITION CHANGES

Decompositional changes are dependent upon the environment. At moderate temperatures, decompositional changes will not occur for a day or two. Then rigor passes, and the body begins to swell and discolor, hair slips off, and marbling forms. By this time, decomposed blood and body fluids come out of the body orifices (called purging). After weeks or months, skeletonization takes place. Occasionally, bodies may decompose more in one part of the body than the other because of injuries, amount of clothing, or intrusion by insects and animals.

ADIPOCERE

This change occurs in a cold, wet environment. The fat tissue beneath skin begins to saponify (turn into soap). It usually takes a minimum of a few weeks to develop, and will keep the body in a relatively preserved state for many months. Unlike normal decompositional changes, there is no green discoloration or significant bloating. The exterior of the body remains white and the outermost layers of the skin slip off. Bodies placed in cold water develop this change. It may also occur in bodies placed in plastic bags.

MUMMIFICATION

Mummification occurs in hot, dry environments. The body dehydrates and bacterial proliferation is minimal. The skin becomes dark, dried, and leathery. The process occurs readily in the fingers and toes in dry environments regardless of the temperature. Most mummified bodies are found in the summer months. It is also common for this process to occur in winter months if the environment is warm. It is possible for an entire body to mummify in a only a few days to weeks. Once a body is in this state, it may remain preserved for many years.

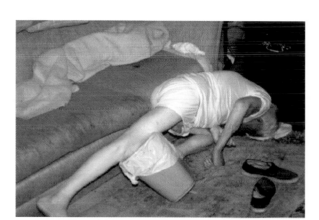

FIGURE 1.1 This man was found in this position the day after he died. His body was completely stiff. This stiffness (rigor mortis) begins in all muscles 1–2 hours after death when the environmental temperature is approximately 75°F. The body will be in complete rigor in 10–12 hours and remain stiff for another 24–36 hours at the same environmental temperature. Heat speeds up the process and cold retards it. See next photo.

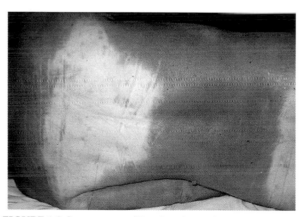

FIGURE 1.3 Livor mortis. Blood settles with gravity after a person dies. The blood becomes fixed in the dependent position in approximately 8–10 hours. Prior to fixation, the blood will redistribute to the new dependent location if the body is moved. The normal color of livor mortis (lividity) is purple. Red lividity can be caused by the cold, cyanide, and carbon monoxide. The lividity in this photo is purple with outlines in red due to refrigeration.

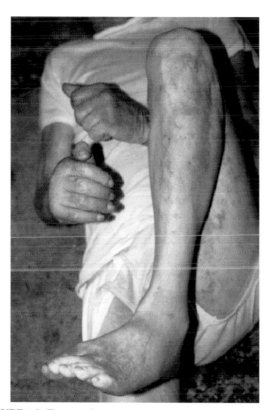

FIGURE 1.2 The man's knee remains bent after he is moved because the rigor mortis is still in a fixed position. It discovered in this position, the examiner would know the body had been moved.

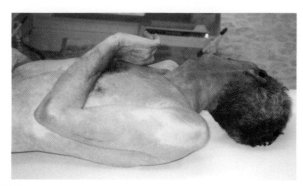

FIGURE 1.4 This man's arm was in complete rigor against his body. See next photo.

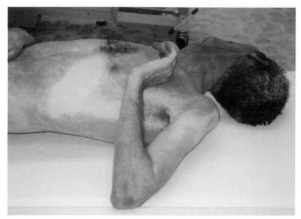

FIGURE 1.5 When the arm is moved, the absence of lividity is apparent where the arm was in contact with the skin.

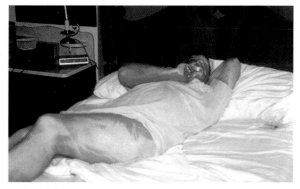

FIGURE 1.6 This man was discovered dead in bed. The pattern of livor mortis suggests the man has been moved after the livor mortis had fixed. See next photo.

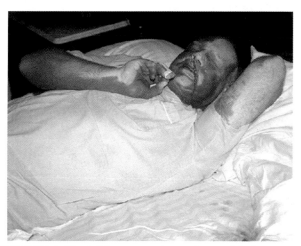

FIGURE 1.7 The lividity pattern is consistent with the man being on his face in the bed. The fluid in the nose matches up with the stained area in the bed.

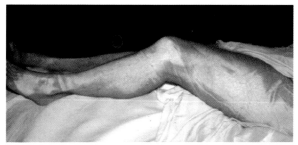

FIGURE 1.8 The pattern of the bedding on the leg suggests the decedent was lying on the bed after death.

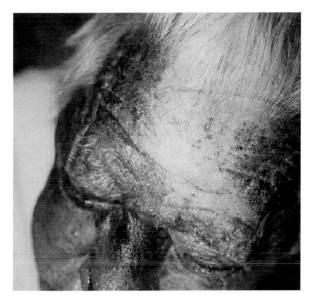

FIGURE 1.9 The pale mark on this man's forehead indicates he was resting on his head after death.

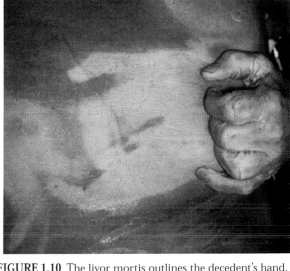

FIGURE 1.10 The livor mortis outlines the decedent's hand. This pattern will not go away since the lividity is fixed.

FIGURE 1.11 Lividity and congestion (buildup of blood) in the head, neck, and upper chest can give this splotchy pattern.

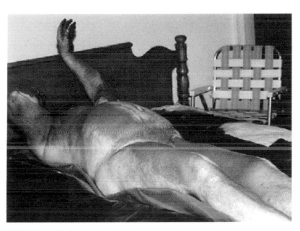

FIGURE 1.12 Both the anterior lividity and the arms fixed up and bent prove this man was rolled over after his body was discovered.

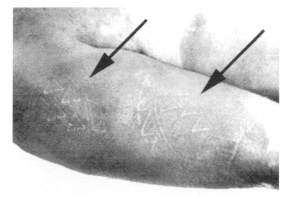

FIGURE 1.13 The arrows point to a shoe pattern on the decedent's arm. There were pale impressions and not bruises or scrapes. This indicates the person was lying against the shoes after death and not before.

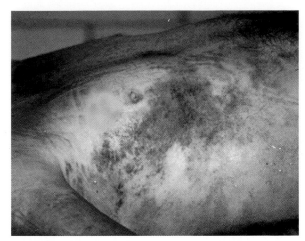

FIGURE 1.14 Occasionally, livor mortis may appear as an unusual pattern or look like an injury. This man was discovered at the bottom of some stairs. The pathologist can cut into the area to differentiate between livor mortis and injury. See next photo.

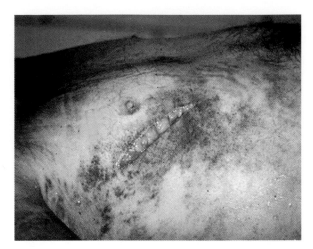

FIGURE 1.15 An incision into the area reveals only the yellow fat and no blood. This indicates the area is lividity and not an injury.

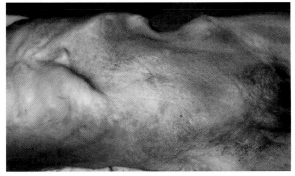

FIGURE 1.16 One of the first signs of decomposition is green discoloration of the skin, especially in the abdomen. Decompositional changes may appear within a few hours if the environmental temperature is high.

FIGURE 1.17 Most bodies turn green during the progression of decomposition. This one did not. The body is swollen (bloated) from bacterial gas formation and there is skin slippage and subcutaneous marbling (the outlines of the blood vessels under the skin).

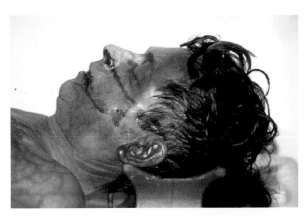

FIGURE 1.18 Internal pressure occurs on the internal organs when gas develops. Pressure pushes bloody fluid out the nose and mouth (purging). This should not be confused with trauma to the nose and mouth.

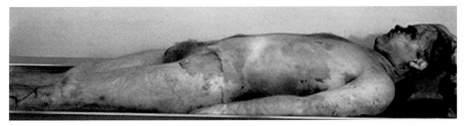

FIGURE 1.19 Bodies may not swell much when they are in hot and dry climates. The skin slippage may also be dry. See next photo.

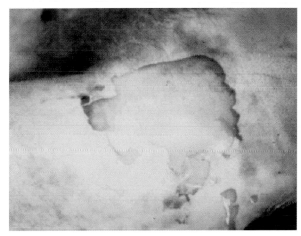

FIGURE 1.20 The skin slippage on the man's hip is dry, not wet and slippery as is usually seen.

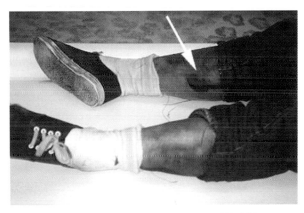

FIGURE 1.21 Skin slippage may cause fluid-filled blisters to occur. These areas should not be confused with thermal injury.

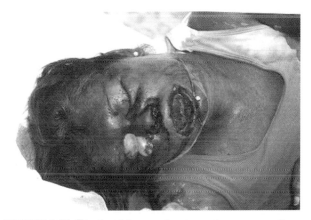

FIGURE 1.22 The facial features begin to change as swelling occurs during decomposition.

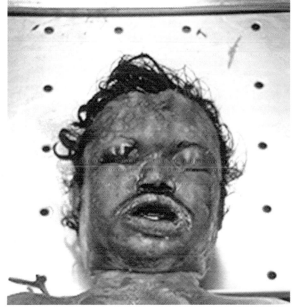

FIGURE 1.23 This man was 21, thin, and white. He was discovered in a river 4–5 days after he was killed in the summertime. Decomposition can cause the facial features to change and the hair to slip off. Visual identification may be difficult when such changes occur.

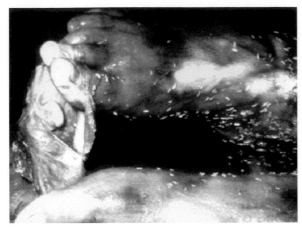

FIGURE 1.24 The skin and toenails have slipped off the feet. If this occurs on the hands, identification could be made with only the slipped-off skin because the fingerprints are on the skin.

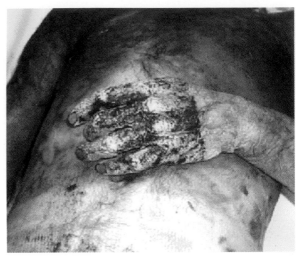

FIGURE 1.25 Notice the difference between the skin of the hand and the rest of the body. This man drowned, leaving the skin of the hands (and feet) wrinkled, in contrast to the skin on the remainder of the body. See next photo.

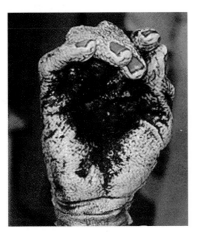

FIGURE 1.26 A close-up view of the hand shows the dramatic wrinkling of the skin. Had the person been in the water longer, the skin might have easily slipped off like a glove.

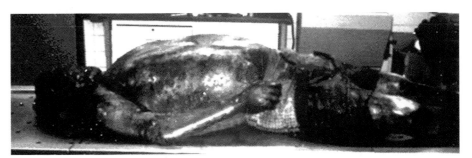

FIGURE 1.27 This 22-year-old white man was found in the woods on a hot summer day five days after he died. The body is markedly swollen and discolored. Initially, he could be mistaken for an African-American man.

FIGURE 1.28 As decomposition continues, the tissues and organs on the inside of the body begin to look the same in color. See next photo.

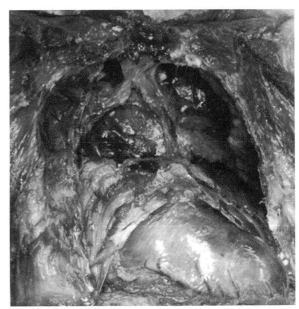

FIGURE 1.29 The internal organs begin to look the same in color as decomposition progresses.

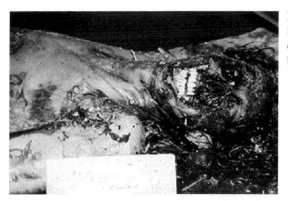

FIGURE 1.30 Three weeks in the winter under a brush pile caused this man's decomposition changes. The head area is more decomposed because he had been shot multiple times there.

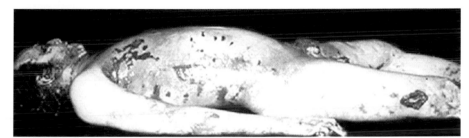

FIGURE 1.31 Except for a few injuries, this man's body is in relatively good shape. He was identified visually. He had been in the water for at least three weeks during February.

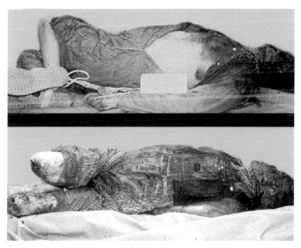

FIGURE 1.32 This man was found on the side of the road two days after he was strangled and beaten in the head. He was also covered with a blanket. See next photo.

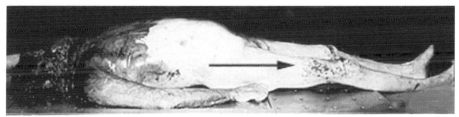

FIGURE 1.33 His body was much more decomposed in the head region where he was injured and less where he was clothed and covered with the blanket. This asymmetrical decomposition is commonly seen when insects and flies are attracted to the blood in the injured areas. Estimating time of death must be done with the least decomposed areas. The arrow points to postmortem insect activity (anthropophagia).

FIGURE 1.34 This is another example of asymmetrical decomposition. The exposed head is much more decomposed than the rest of the body, which is in the sleeping bag.

FIGURE 1.35 The next series of photos are of a man shot in the back of the head and buried. He was discovered six months after burial. See next photo.

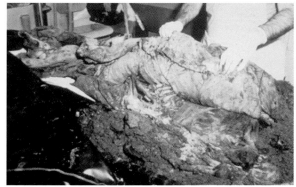

FIGURE 1.36 Much of the surrounding dirt accompanied the body. The blanket wrapping the body was carefully removed. The remains and the dirt had already been X-rayed. No bullets were discovered.

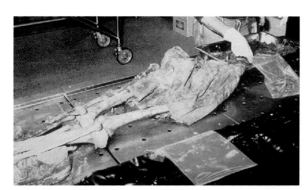

FIGURE 1.37 There was no soft tissue remaining. A dentist was asked to look through all of the bone fragments of the face and head in order to find some teeth for identification. He was unsuccessful. See next photo.

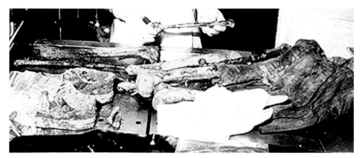

FIGURE 1.38 The skeleton was complete except for the head. Many of the facial fragments were lost at the time of the shooting. The man was wearing red shoes, shorts, and a shirt which were used in the identification. See next photo.

FIGURE 1.39 This is the trunk area. The T-shirt he was wearing helped to identify him.

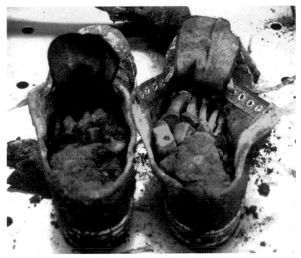

FIGURE 1.40 The bones of the feet were still in the red sport shoes.

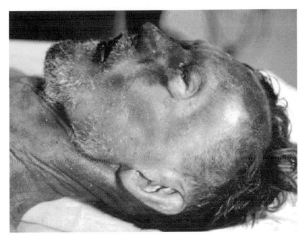

FIGURE 1.41 Mummification. The skin dries out and turns leathery. This man's head mummified within two days because his head was next to a heater. His head will not decompose further due to the mummification. See next photo.

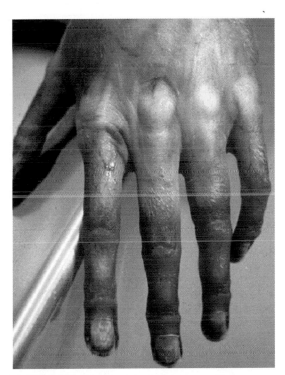

FIGURE 1.42 His hands had also mummified.

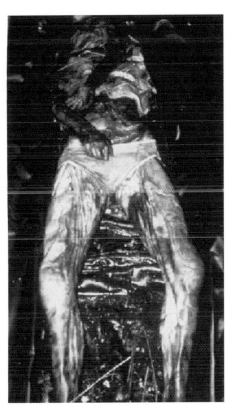

FIGURE 1.43 These remains were completely mummified in approximately six weeks during the summer months.

FIGURE 1.44 Adipocere. A clothed body wrapped in a U-Haul blanket was discovered at the edge of a lake. See next photo.

FIGURE 1.45 The body was still white and originally thought by law enforcement to not be very decomposed. They thought the body had been in the water about a week. See next photo.

FIGURE 1.46 Upon closer examination the skin appeared to be thickened with the superficial layers of the skin missing. This change is called adipocere. The soft tissue turns into a soap-like substance (saponification). This occurs in cold wet conditions. Once the change occurs it will remain for years. See next photo.

FIGURE 1.47 Even though she had been in the cold water for over ten months, she was visually identified by the sheriff. See next photo.

FIGURE 1.48 She was also identified by numerous tattoos. See next photo.

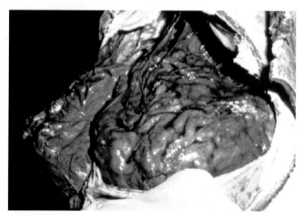

FIGURE 1.49 The internal organs were in remarkably good condition given the time in the water. This photograph of the brain shows that it was still in good enough condition to be examined for evidence of trauma.

FIGURE 1.50 This case is another example of adipocere. The body was buried for more than two years in a casket which filled with water. See next photo.

FIGURE 1.51 The remains are much less preserved than in the previous case. An examination could be made; however, the results were not as good as hoped.

FIGURE 1.52 This woman was in cold water for approximately three months. Adipocere was only beginning. Adipocere change usually takes months before it is well-developed. The mark on the neck is from a cable (tied to a concrete block) which aided in sinking the body.

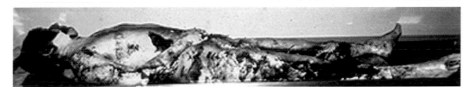

FIGURE 1.53 The black discoloration on the skin is mold. This man had been embalmed and buried for over three years. See next photo.

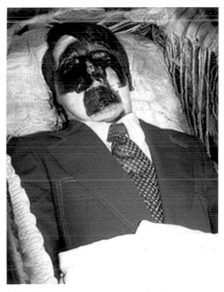

FIGURE 1.54 The man in the casket. Aside from the mold, the body was well-preserved. See next photo.

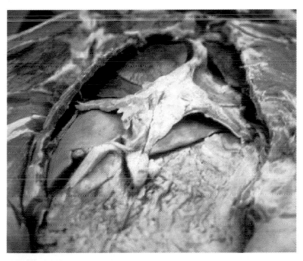

FIGURE 1.55 The internal organs were in very good condition and could be easily evaluated.

FIGURE 1.56 This man's body was disinterred because a faulty heart valve was thought to be the cause of his death. See next photo.

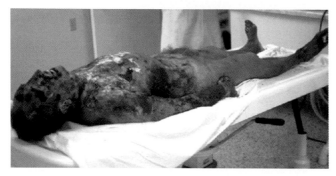

FIGURE 1.57 The body had undergone moderate change with mold on the external surface and internal organ softening and discoloration. See next photo.

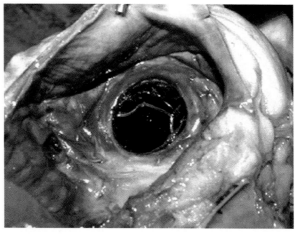

FIGURE 1.58 The heart valve could easily be located and evaluated. In this case, the valve did not malfunction; however, it was damaged from the trocarring performed during the embalming process.

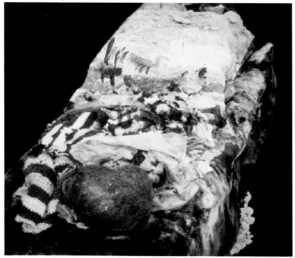

FIGURE 1.59 This woman's body was placed in a steel box, filled with concrete, and buried under the house. The concrete did not totally encase the body because her back was lying on the bottom of the box. She was found approximately 18 months after death. See next photo.

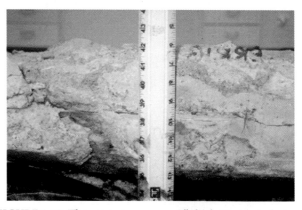

FIGURE 1.60 The concrete was over 7" thick. See next photo.

FIGURE 1.61 The body had markedly decomposed while in the concrete for almost two years. No cause of death could be proven. There were no fractures. The woman was thought to have been strangled.

FIGURE 1.63 After ten days in the ground the body was in relatively good condition. See next photo.

FIGURE 1.62 A woman was abducted, killed, and buried here out in the woods. See next photo.

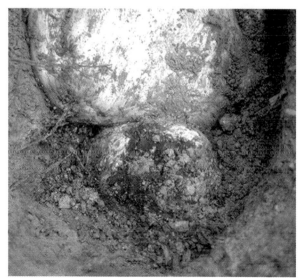

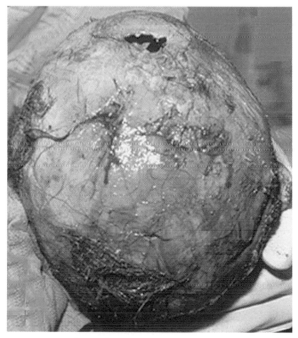

FIGURE 1.64 There was obvious trauma to the head. The body was transported directly to the morgue and placed in refrigeration. See next photo.

FIGURE 1.65 This is the top of her head. There were marked decompositional changes by the time the autopsy was performed the next day.

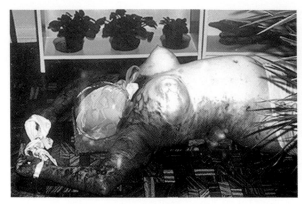

FIGURE 1.66 This woman was suffocated two days prior to being found. Notice the color change, including the subcutaneous marbling of the skin. See next photo.

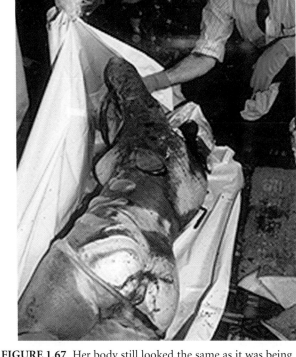

FIGURE 1.67 Her body still looked the same as it was being removed to the morgue. See next photo.

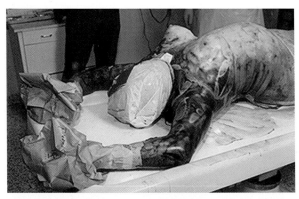

FIGURE 1.68 The body had a completely different color the next day at the autopsy. Bodies may change from the time of discovery and scene investigation to the autopsy. This is especially true if the bodies are transported over long distances to the morgue.

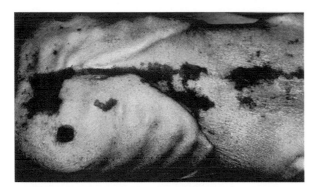

FIGURE 1.69 The abraded lesions were caused by roaches after death. This is called anthropophagia.

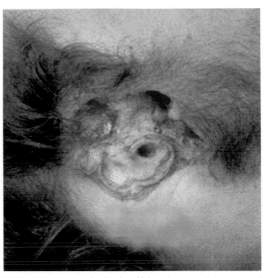

FIGURE 1.70 Notice the lack of blood around the area where the ear is missing. A rat had chewed off this man's ear after he died in a car.

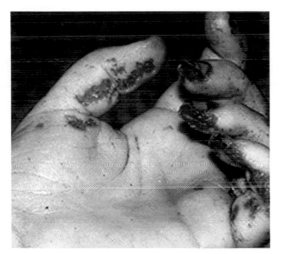

FIGURE 1.71 Most postmortem injuries are usually red-brown to brown with a lack of blood in or around the wounds. However, they may be red if the area is in a dependent position.

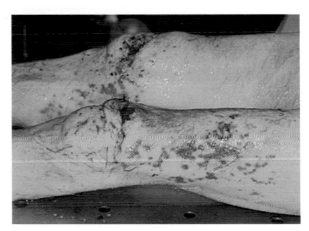

FIGURE 1.72 These injuries were caused by insects. The man was clothed and wrapped in a blanket. The injuries are somewhat more red than usual.

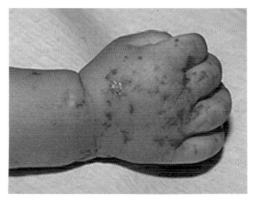

FIGURE 1.73 Another example of anthropophagia by ants or roaches. This baby was thought to have been abused because an emergency room (ER) physician saw these marks and became suspicious. The child died of SIDS.

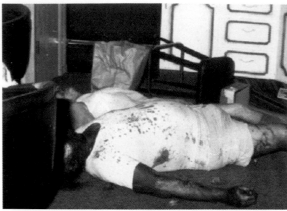

FIGURE 1.74 A couple with a handicapped son was visited every week by a visiting nurse who worked with the son. She came for her weekly visit and discovered the couple on the kitchen floor. See next photo.

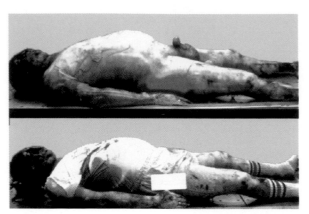

FIGURE 1.75 The man had been dead for 4–5 days. The degree of his body's decomposition was consistent with the mail and newspaper buildup outside the house. Autopsy revealed significant coronary artery disease as a cause of death. See next photo.

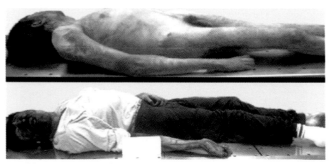

FIGURE 1.76 The son was not as decomposed as the father and his lividity was cherry red. Autopsy revealed physical deformities (he was confined to a wheelchair), a carbon monoxide level of 30% and no other cause for his death. See next photo.

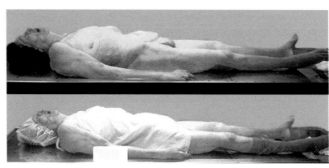

FIGURE 1.77 The mother's body was not decomposed. Autopsy revealed cardiomegaly, pericarditis, and aortic stenosis. Toxicology was negative for all drugs, including the digoxin she was supposed to be taking. See next photo.

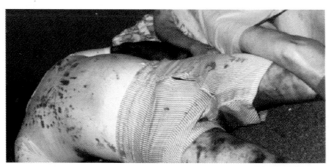

FIGURE 1.78 A closer look at the original scene shows the wife with her leg over her husband's leg. The only thing out of place at the scene was an overturned stool next to the bodies. A car in the garage was empty of gas and the key was in the "on" position. See next photo.

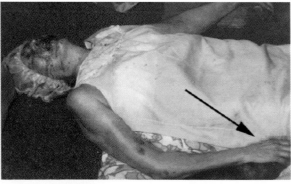

FIGURE 1.79 In summary. The father died first of heart disease. The wife killed the son by carbon monoxide in the garage and then killed herself. At the end, she laid next to her husband, grabbed his hand (arrow), and waited for death. Their physician confirmed the fact that the husband and wife had a suicide pact; if one of them died, the other would kill the son and then commit suicide.

Chapter 2

IDENTIFICATION (I.D.)

POSITIVE IDENTIFICATION (I.D.)

Visual

Even though this method of identification is the most common and easiest, problems may be encountered. Numerous injuries and decompositional changes may cause such disfigurement that the family may not take a good enough look to make sure this is or is not their relative.

Fingerprints

Little needs to be said about this method of identification because of the uniqueness of fingerprints for each individual.

Dental

Unless the decedent is edentulous, dental comparison is an excellent method for making a positive identification because most people have had some type of dental work. Many times, decedents with a set of dentures can be identified. The technician who made the dentures may put the decedent's name or some other form of personal identification on the denture.

X-rays

Antemortem studies can be used for postmortem comparisons. X-rays of the skull and the pelvis tend to be the best for comparison. The skull has sinuses (cavities) which are specific for each individual. A chest X-ray is not as good as the skull and pelvis for comparison.

DNA Fingerprinting

All individuals except identical twins have different DNA sequences on their chromosomes. These DNA sequences can be broken down and studied by the use of enzymes. The procedures for performing these tests were developed in the 1980s, making them relatively new. Any material with cells containing DNA can be used for comparison. Blood, hair, semen, teeth, and other tissue may be used.

PRESUMPTIVE IDENTIFICATION (I.D.)

Skeletal Remains

Skeletal remains are usually examined by an anthropologist — hopefully, a forensic anthropologist. Such professionals are expert in estimating age, gender, and race, and may use numerous scientific formulae to arrive at their conclusions. Age estimations are the most difficult to make; however, this determination is becoming easier now that microscopic analyses are being performed.

Clothing

The style, size, and make of clothing are commonly used to make a presumptive identification. Relatives or friends may remember what the missing person was last wearing. Unfortunately, many clothes will decompose along with the rest of the body or they will become destroyed if the body is burned.

X-rays

The location of antemortem X-rays does not ensure a positive identification can be made. There may not be enough points of variation allowing the radiologist to render a conclusive opinion. A presumptive identification can be made if the X-rays are consistent with those of the decedent, and there is no reason to believe the person is anyone else.

Physical Features

Tattoos, scars, birthmarks, the absence of organs from surgical procedures, and other physical anomalies are helpful in making identifications. The presence or absence of any of these characteristics may also be helpful in eliminating any possible matches, as well as making a possible identification.

Circumstances Surrounding Death

Identifications may be impossible to make based on the few remains discovered at the scene; however, the circumstances in which the remains are discovered may allow an identification to be made. For example, if only a few pieces of a body are located in a burned-out house, an identification cannot be made based on any scientific testing. But, if the owner of the house was last seen in the house, or if there is no other reason to believe the remains are those of someone else, a presumptive identification of the owner can still be made.

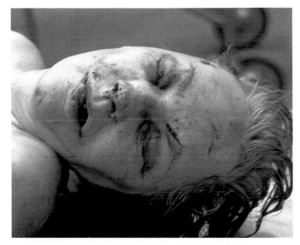

FIGURE 2.1 This woman's face was traumatized due to a motor vehicle accident. Care must be taken when asking the family for a visual identification (I.D.). Many family members or friends are hesitant to give a positive I.D. when the face has been injured.

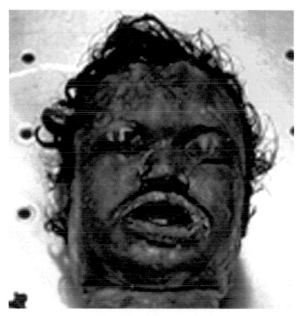

FIGURE 2.2 Visual identification may also be difficult in cases in which the decedent's body has undergone moderate decomposition. This is the face of a thin, white man in his early twenties after being in the water for five days in the summertime.

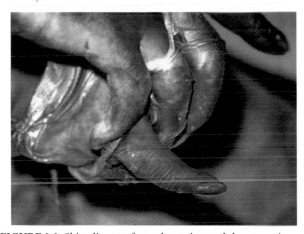

FIGURE 2.3 Skin slippage from drowning and decomposition. Skin may also slip off due to the heat. Only the skin is needed to take a fingerprint. See next photos.

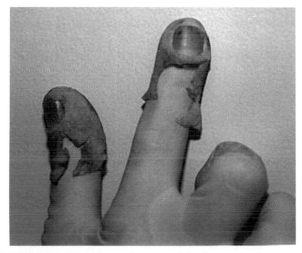

FIGURE 2.4 The skin on the ends of the fingers can be removed for printing. See next photo.

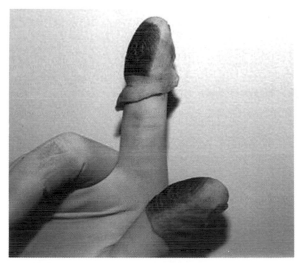

FIGURE 2.5 This skin can easily be printed.

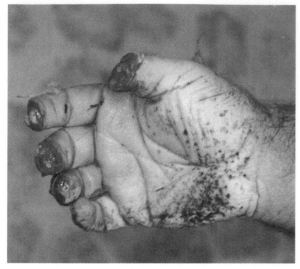

FIGURE 2.6 If necessary, the ends of the fingers or the entire hand may be removed and sent to the lab for printing.

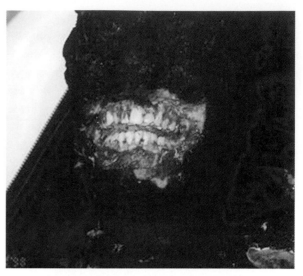

FIGURE 2.7 The teeth may withstand extensive thermal injury and decomposition. Even though this body is charred, the teeth remain a good source for identification.

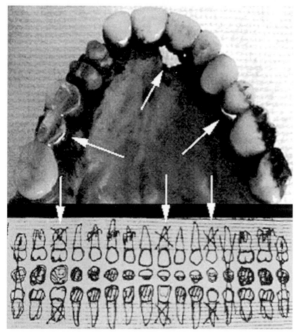

FIGURE 2.8 Teeth are compared to the dental chart for identification. There are numerous points of positive matches (arrows) in this case.

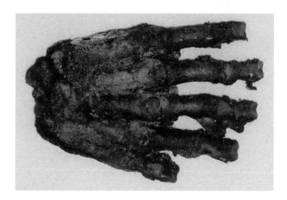

FIGURE 2.9 This "hand" specimen was discovered in a dumpster. Law enforcement was worried this may be part of a homicide. Notice there is only one smaller digit. See next photo.

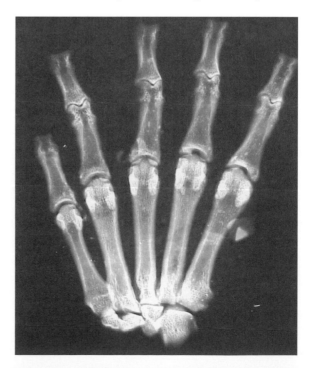

FIGURE 2.10 Further examination of the hand and the X-ray revealed the specimen to be a bear paw. A local taxidermist threw the specimen in the dumpster.

FIGURE 2.11 In charred bodies, most of the skin may be burned off the bone and only the saw is needed to remove the mandible and maxilla for identification. See next photo.

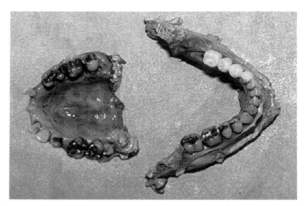

FIGURE 2.12 Once removed, the maxilla (left) and the mandible can now be easily examined, photographed, and X-rayed.

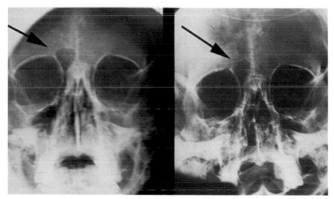

FIGURE 2.13 These are antemortem and postmortem comparisons useful for identifying a skull. An X-ray from a previous traffic accident (left) was compared to a postmortem radiograph. The arrows point to the frontal sinus on each which match. This finding makes a positive match. This skull was discovered with other parts of a skeleton. The police thought they knew the decedent's identity; however, a positive match had to be made.

FIGURE 2.14 This body was discovered in a field. It was thought to be that of an African-American man who was shot in the abdomen during a barroom brawl. In order to prosecute the assailant, a positive I.D. needed to be made. See next photo.

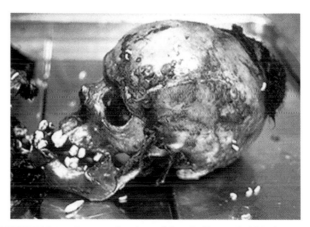

FIGURE 2.15 An examination of the skull revealed black curly hair and the jaw of a man. The teeth appeared as though no dentist had ever worked on them. The findings were consistent with those of an African-American man; however, positive proof must be made. See next photo.

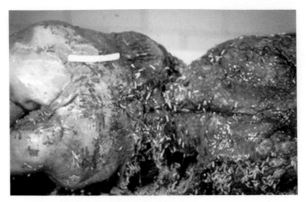

FIGURE 2.16 There was moderate decomposition to the torso with abundant maggots. Notice the difference in the degree of decompositional changes between the torso and the skull in the previous photo. See next photo.

FIGURE 2.17 The clothing was consistent with those worn by the man when he was shot. This is still not enough for a positive I.D. See next photo.

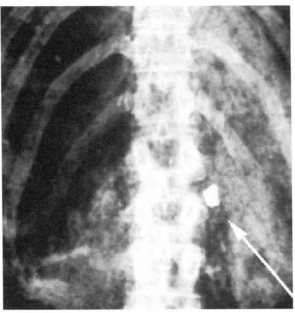

FIGURE 2.18 A postmortem X-ray revealed a bullet (arrow) next to the spine. The man had recently been shot because examination revealed no scar tissue around the bullet. See next photo.

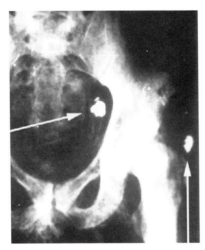

FIGURE 2.19 An X-ray of the pelvis revealed bullet fragments. These were surrounded by scar tissue, indicating the man had been shot before. See next photo.

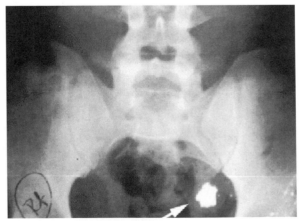

FIGURE 2.20 An eight-year-old X-ray from the probable victim revealed the same fragments as seen on the postmortem radiograph. See next photo.

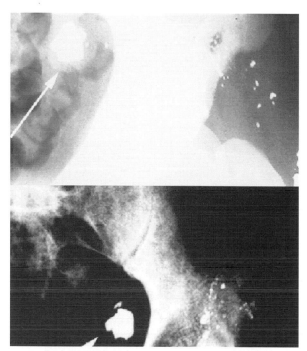

FIGURE 2.21 A comparison of the two X-rays revealed not only a match with the bullet fragments, but also a match of the pelvic bones. Now a positive I.D. can be made and the assailant brought to trial.

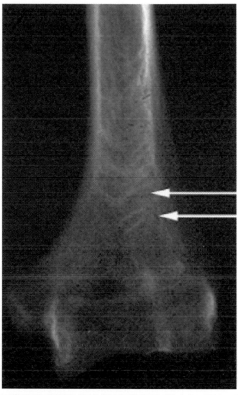

FIGURE 2.22 Small growth lines (Harris lines) within the bone (arrows) are unique. No two individuals will have the same pattern(s).

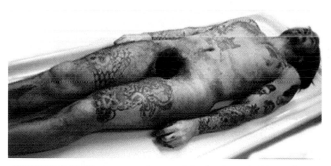

FIGURE 2.23 Tattoos may be good for both probable and positive I.D.s. Occasionally the tattoo artists are able to identify their work.

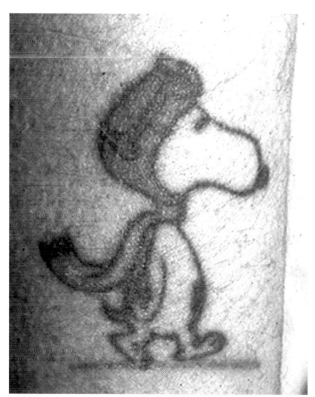

FIGURE 2.24 Some tattoos are cute, but may not be very unique. However, they might aid in the decedent's eventual identification.

FIGURE 2.25 Rarely will tattoos such as these not be linked to a particular person.

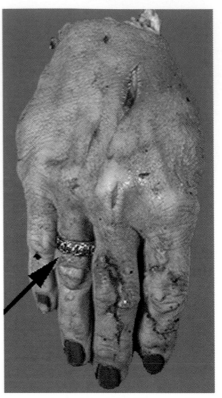

FIGURE 2.26 The ring on this lady's finger was the only evidence allowing the woman's identification to be made after a plane crash. This was good enough for a positive I.D. because her son readily identified the ring.

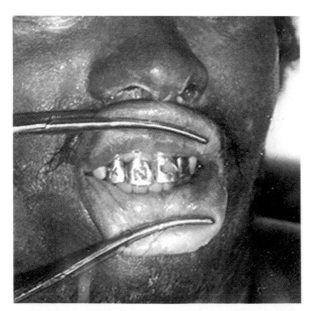

FIGURE 2.27 The gold caps with initials make this identification relatively easy.

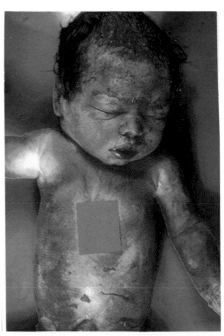

FIGURE 2.28 This baby was discovered in a toilet. His identification was made with DNA testing. Prior to this technology, the baby's identity may not have been solved.

Chapter 3

BLUNT TRAUMA

GENERAL

The characteristic injuries of blunt trauma are contusions, abrasions, and lacerations. Abrasions occur externally whereas contusions and lacerations may be external or internal.

Contusions (Bruises)

Contusions are discolorations of the skin caused by bleeding into the tissues from ruptured blood vessels. In general, the older a person, the easier the vessels will rupture. There is no way, however, to determine exactly how much force is needed to produce a contusion. The age of a contusion is difficult to determine because of the great variability of a body's reaction to trauma. People with blood disorders and liver disease may develop more severe contusions than healthy individuals. As healing occurs, a contusion changes color from blue or red, to red-blue, to green, to brown, and finally yellow. These color changes, however, may appear out of order and may overlap. There is no way to know how long each color stage will last. Occasionally a recent contusion will have a brown tinge.

Abrasions (Scrapes)

An abrasion is denuded skin caused by friction. A wound may be either deep or superficial depending on the force and the coarseness of the surface which caused the abrasion. A person who slides across pavement might have a deeper and rougher wound than a person who slides across a rug. Occasionally, the direction of the force can be determined. If one end of a wound has margins with raised skin, for example, the force originated from the opposite side.

Lacerations (Tears)

Tears of the skin from blunt trauma are called lacerations. Many tears are associated with both contusions and abrasions. For example, a blow to the head with a hammer may cause tearing of the scalp with adjacent abrasions. If blood escapes into the surrounding tissues, the skin can also be bruised.

A laceration must be distinguished from a cutting injury. A laceration usually has bridges of tissue connecting one side of the wound to the other. Cutting and incised wounds have no tissue bridges because a sharp object cuts the wound cleanly from the top to the bottom of the wound.

Deaths due to blunt trauma may have some or none of the above external signs of trauma. This is particularly true of fatal blows to the abdomen.

BLUNT HEAD TRAUMA

Blunt trauma to the scalp and face can produce contusions, lacerations, and abrasions. However, there may be no external signs of trauma to the head if a person has a full head of hair. Obvious external injuries are not necessary for a death to be caused by head trauma. Occasionally, the weapon leaves a characteristic identifying pattern on the scalp. Unfortunately, this is the exception rather than the rule.

Battle's sign — a bluish discoloration of the skin behind the ear that occurs from blood leaking under the scalp after a skull fracture.

Spectacle hemorrhage (raccoon's eyes) — a discoloration of the tissues around the eyes usually due to a fracture of the skull. The hemorrhages may involve one or both eyes and may be mistakenly interpreted that the decedent had been struck about the face and eyes.

When a person receives a significant blow to the head there will be bleeding under the scalp even if there are no external injuries. Depending on the amount of force there may be skull fractures. There are many different types of skull fractures; however, the specific type is not as important as recognizing a pattern such as a circular fracture caused by a hammer.

There are three major types of hemorrhages which occur in the skull. The type of hemorrhage helps the examiner understand what may have caused death.

1) **Epidural hemorrhage** — bleeding directly under the skull on top of the dura mater. It is associated with a skull fracture and a torn artery. This type of hemorrhage accumulates rapidly and death may occur quickly.

2) **Subdural hemorrhage** — bleeding under dura mater on top of the brain. It may or may not be associated with trauma and is caused by torn veins which forces the blood to accumulate more slowly than the epidural bleed.

3) **Subarachnoid hemorrhage** — caused by blunt trauma or ruptured blood vessels. It is located directly on the surface of the brain.

Pathologists also look for the presence of coup and contrecoup injuries to the brain to help differentiate between a fall and a blow to the head by a second party.

Coup injury — caused when a moving object (such as a hammer) strikes a stationary head. The injuries to the brain will be directly beneath the point where the weapon strikes the head.

Contrecoup injury — caused when a moving head (as in a fall) strikes a stationary object like the floor. The injuries to the brain will be opposite the point of impact.

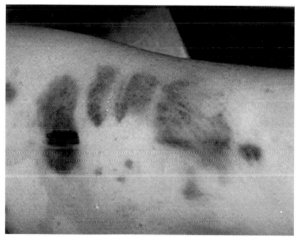

FIGURE 3.1 The bruises on this woman's arm appear as if made by fingers. The man who killed the woman made the bruises. There is no way to determine the size of the hand or the strength it took to cause the bruises.

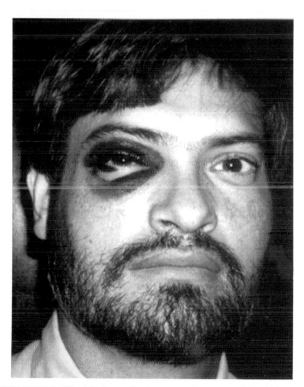

FIGURE 3.2 The black eye looks recent because of its color. It is one week old. People bruise and heal differently. Determining the age of a bruise is difficult.

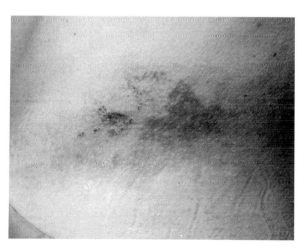

FIGURE 3.3 Bruises (contusions) change color as they heal. They may progress from red/blue, green, brown to yellow, as they heal. Unfortunately, all contusions do not resolve the same. The multicolored bruise in this photograph is exactly one week old.

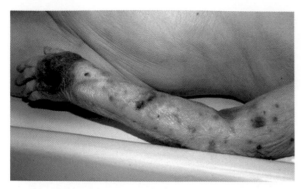

FIGURE 3.4 Older people bruise easily. They may have many bruises of the arms and legs. These are not necessarily suspicious.

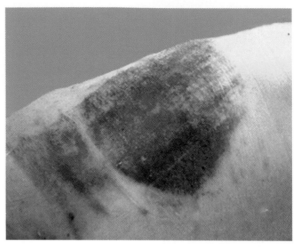

FIGURE 3.5 The scraping away of the skin is an abrasion. The direction the body was traveling when the injury was received can be determined if the skin is heaped up on one edge.

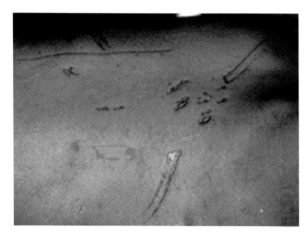

FIGURE 3.6 Brown and yellow injuries with no bleeding are postmortem injuries. The injuries to this woman's back occurred after her death from head trauma.

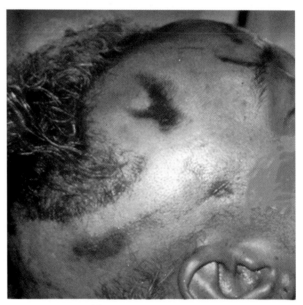

FIGURE 3.7 Most blunt impact injuries do not leave a distinct enough pattern for the examiner to prove the type of weapon used.

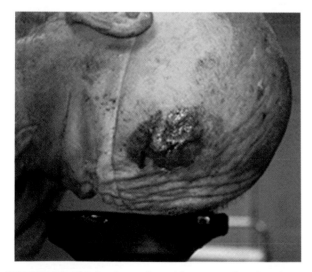

FIGURE 3.8 This is a laceration with surrounding abrasion and contusion. The man fell and hit his head while he was dying from heart disease.

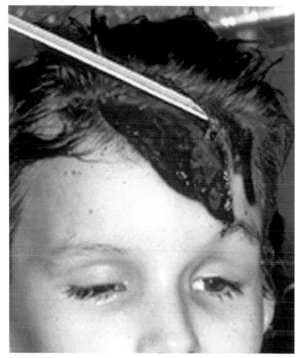

FIGURE 3.9 The direction from which a blow to the head came can be determined by "undermining." The side of the wound which can be lifted off the bone is the undermined side. In this photograph, the ruler is placed under the scalp on the left side. This is the undermined side, indicating the blow came from the right side.

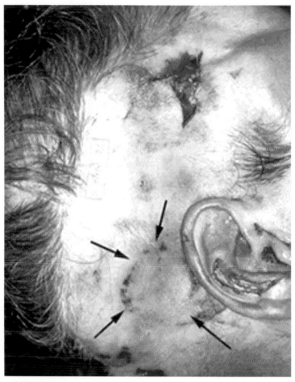

FIGURE 3.10 This man was struck in the head multiple times with a large hammer. All three signs of blunt trauma are visible. The arrows outline the pattern of the hammer.

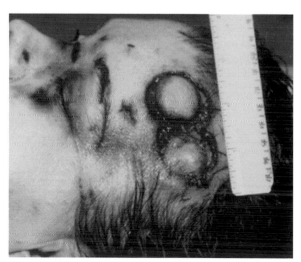

FIGURE 3.11 This woman had two cookie cutter-like wounds which appear as if they were made by a pipe. Unfortunately, the weapon was never located. See next photo.

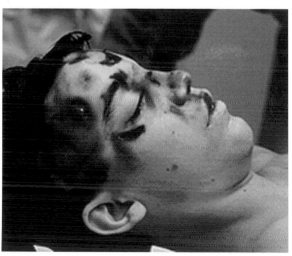

FIGURE 3.12 The woman's son was beaten with the same object; however, the patterns were not quite as obvious. See next photo.

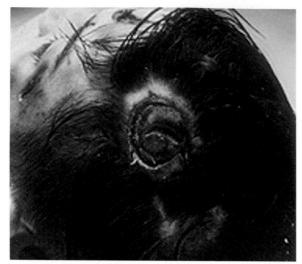

FIGURE 3.13 The wounds to his head were similar to his mother's wounds, but his were overlapping.

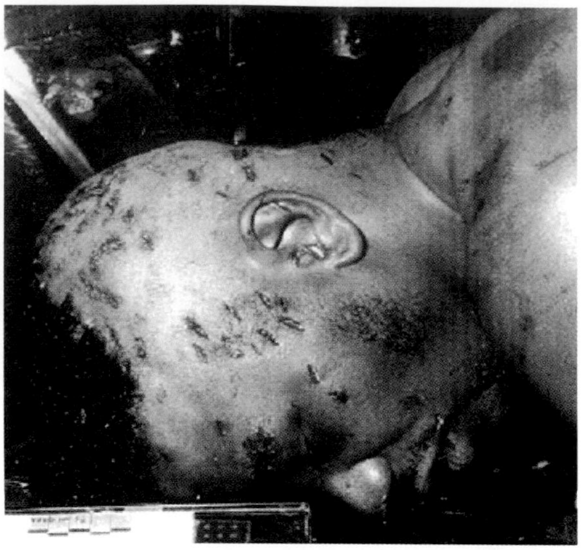

FIGURE 3.14 The multiple blows to this man's head were caused by the claw end of a hammer.

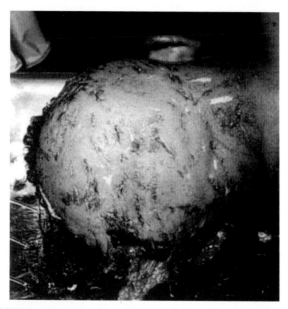

FIGURE 3.15 More claw injuries on the head from a hammer.

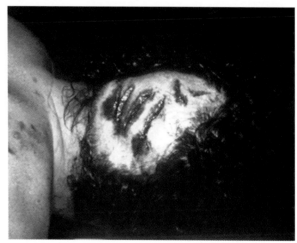

FIGURE 3.16 There were multiple lacerations on this man's head. There was no pattern. Looking at the rest of the body gave clues as to the origin of the tears. See next photo.

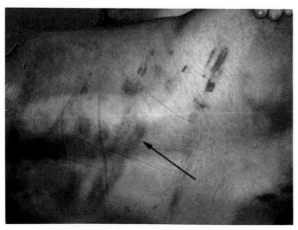

FIGURE 3.17 The contusions to his back were long with pale centers. When a long, thin, heavy object strikes the body, the point of impact may be pale and the edges will be bruised. See next photo.

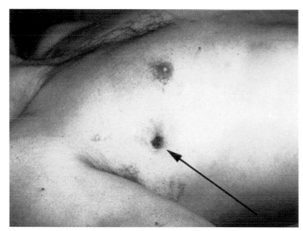

FIGURE 3.18 The man died from a gunshot wound to the chest. The marks on the back were caused by blows from the barrel of the rifle and the lacerations of the head were caused by blows from the stock.

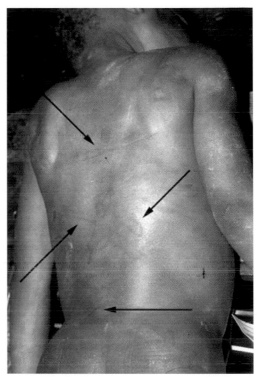

FIGURE 3.19 This child was struck multiple times on the front and back of the trunk. He died of a ruptured liver. See next photo.

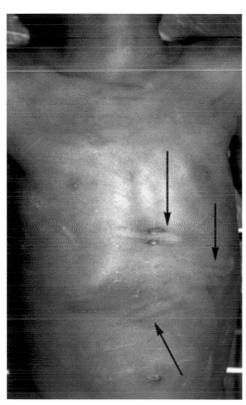

FIGURE 3.20 The injuries to the back were similar to those on the front. They were caused by a thin object which left linear marks, some of which had pale centers. The assailant said he used a belt.

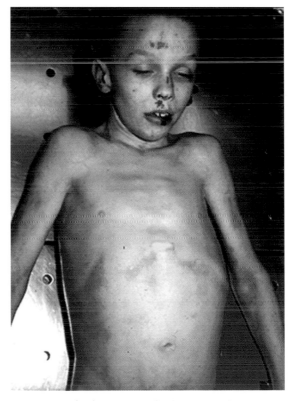

FIGURE 3.21 This boy was involved in an accident. There were no obvious external injuries. See next photo.

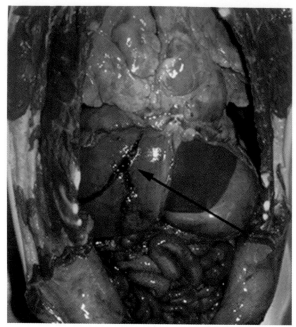

FIGURE 3.22 He died from a blow to the abdomen which caused lacerations of the liver. It is important to note there were no external signs of injury.

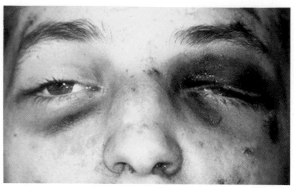

FIGURE 3.23 This boy has spectacle hemorrhages. The black eyes may occur from a direct blow to the eyes, side of the head, or from blood seeping down around the eyes after fractures of the skull. If there are no injuries around the eyes then the hemorrhages probably came from fractures of the skull.

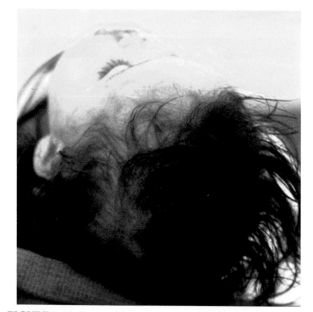

FIGURE 3.24 External injuries may not be present even if someone dies of head trauma. This child reportedly fell and struck his head. See next photo.

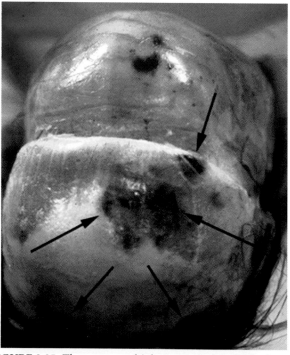

FIGURE 3.25 There were multiple areas of subscalpular hemorrhage which indicate the child was struck in the head and did not fall.

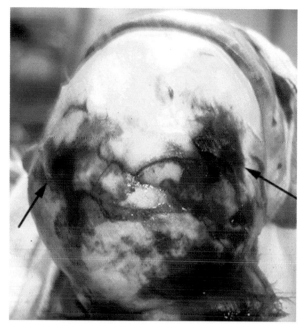

FIGURE 3.26 The blood on the skull (arrows) indicates separate blows to the head.

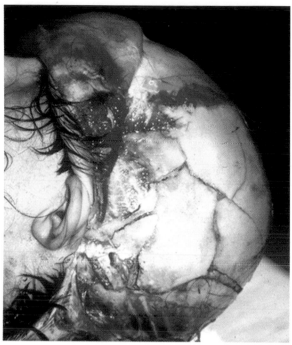

FIGURE 3.27 Many fractures indicate more than one blow to the head; however, unless there are definable points of impact, the examiner must not "guess" as to the number of blows.

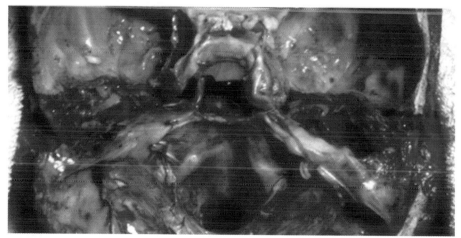

FIGURE 3.28 Fractures of the skull signify at least one blunt impact injury. The fracture at the base of the skull in this case is called a "hinged" fracture because the front and back of the skull can be moved like a hinge.

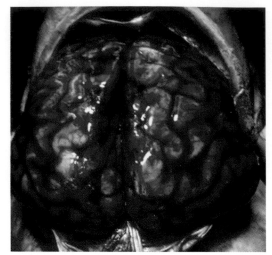

FIGURE 3.29 Subarachnoid hemorrhage. When a blood vessel ruptures over the base of the brain the blood accumulates
on both sides of the brain. This can be readily observed as
soon as the skull and dura mater are removed. See next photo.

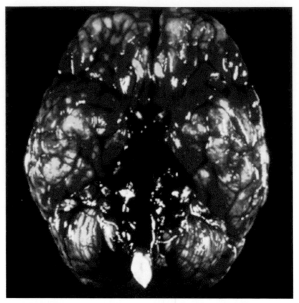

FIGURE 3.30 A ruptured cerebral aneurysm (a ballooned-out
artery) will cause massive bleeding over the base of the brain.

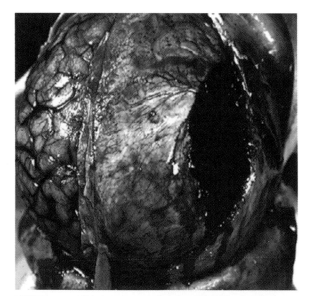

FIGURE 3.31 This is an example of epidural hemorrhage.
The blood accumulates on the outside of the dura mater. The
bleeding usually has a disk shape and it originates by the rupture of an artery. There is usually a fracture of the skull.

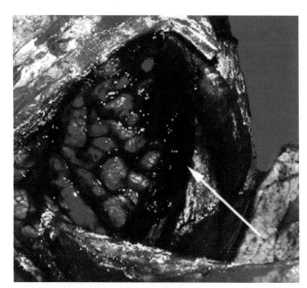

FIGURE 3.32 A subdural hemorrhage is blood under the
dura. It originates from ruptured veins. There may not be an
associated fracture of the skull.

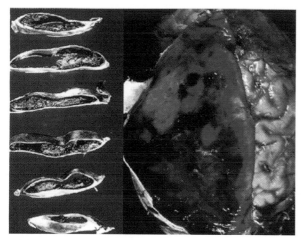

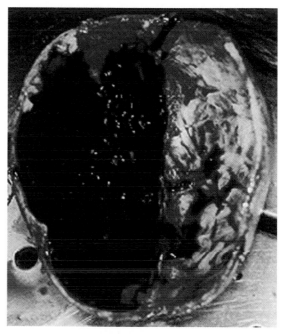

FIGURE 3.33 An old subdural hemorrhage may be discovered incidentally during an autopsy. The healed area of bleeding may become encapsulated (left) and can be removed, leaving only a space.

FIGURE 3.34 Subdural hemorrhage on the base of the skull of at least two days' duration. The brain has been removed.

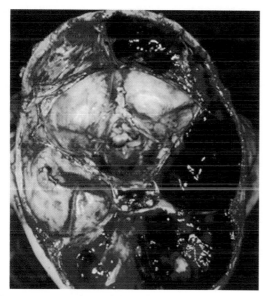

FIGURE 3.35 Another subdural hemorrhage seen after removal of the brain.

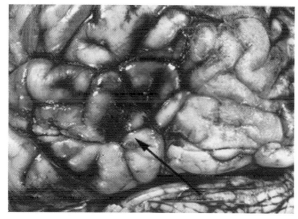

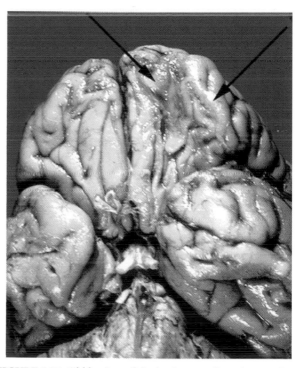

FIGURE 3.36 A red/brown contusion of the brain.

FIGURE 3.37 Old bruises of the brain are yellow depressed lesions (arrows). Recent bruises are red to brown.

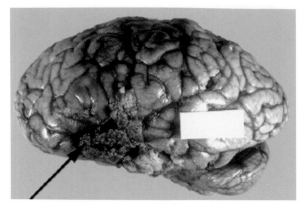

FIGURE 3.38 Contusions of the brain from a hammer blow.

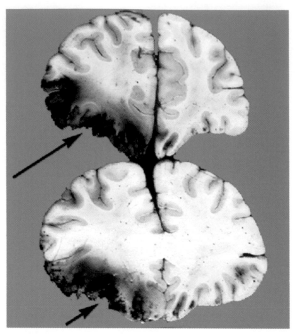

FIGURE 3.39 There are extensive injuries to this brain (arrow) from blows to the head. These injuries would be considered coup injuries if there were signs of external trauma on the same side as the brain injuries.

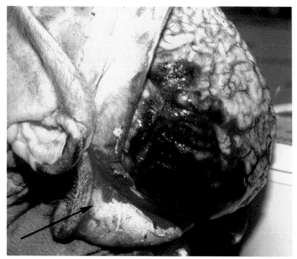

FIGURE 3.40 This is contrecoup injury to the brain. The overlying scalp and bone are not injured (arrow), indicating the blow was on the opposite side of the head.

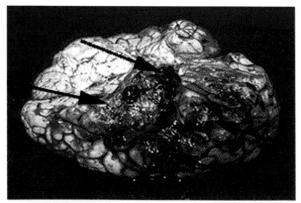

FIGURE 3.41 Multiple coup contusions and lacerations of the brain caused by a heavy weapon.

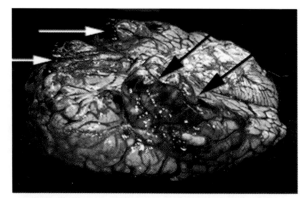

FIGURE 3.42 Coup and contrecoup injuries in a traffic accident. Sometimes recreating the scene and how the person received the injuries may be difficult, if not impossible.

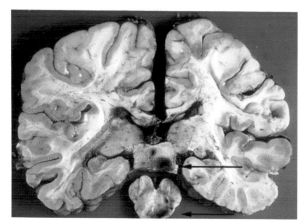

FIGURE 3.43 Intermediate contusions. The contusions (arrows) occurred when the decedent was ejected from the car and struck the top of his head on a tree.

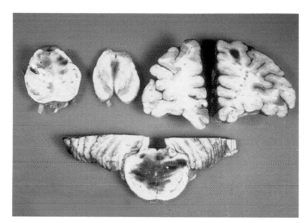

FIGURE 3.44 More intermediate contusions occurring after a blow to the top of the head while the head was in motion.

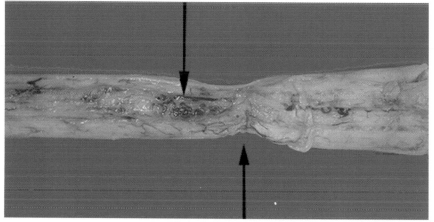

FIGURE 3.45 Injuries to the spinal cord may be obvious with prominent hemorrhage or they may only appear as a softening caused by bone impingement. Most victims of spinal cord injury who die do not have a "broken" neck because the bones of the vertebral column slip over each other and do not break (subluxation).

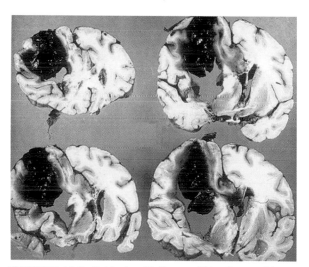

FIGURE 3.46 Individuals with liver and bleeding problems may have bleeding complications days after the trauma. The bleeding in this brain occurred five days after the decedent was struck in the head.

Chapter 4

BLUNT TRAUMA CASES

FIGURE 4.1 Determining the manner of death in falls from great heights may be difficult. See next photo.

FIGURE 4.2 The body of a young man was discovered on the ground at the base of this cliff directly beneath the investigator wearing the yellow jacket. See next photo.

FIGURE 4.3 There were few visible external injuries to the body. Autopsy revealed significant head trauma. See next photo.

FIGURE 4.4 The manner of death was determined in part by the finding of an old scar and a recent incised wound on the decedent's right wrist. Investigation also revealed the decedent had been despondent.

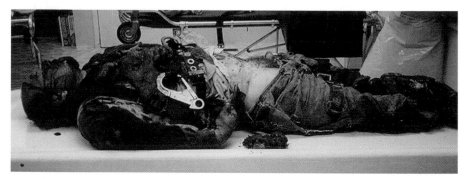

FIGURE 4.5 This man was working on a tower when he fell over 200' to his death. He had numerous injuries to his trunk and extremities. See next photo.

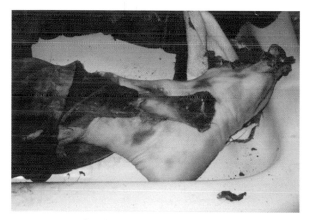

FIGURE 4.6 He landed with such force that some of his long bones came through the skin. See next photo.

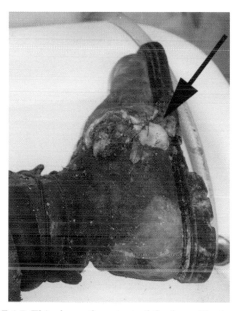

FIGURE 4.7 This shows the extent of the force. The bone came through his boot.

FIGURE 4.8 A man was found dead on the sidewalk with massive head trauma. See next photo.

FIGURE 4.9 On top of the building above the decedent, a pulley device with counterweights had been knocked over by high winds. See next photo.

FIGURE 4.10 This is the metal counterweight which fell off the building and struck the man in the head.

FIGURE 4.11 This man fell at his home. The impressive amount of blood at the scene proves his death was not sudden. See next photo.

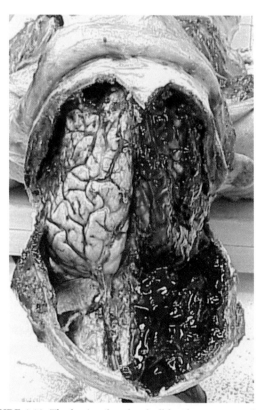

FIGURE 4.12 The brain after the skull has been removed. Both a subdural hemorrhage and contrecoup contusions were present. See next photo.

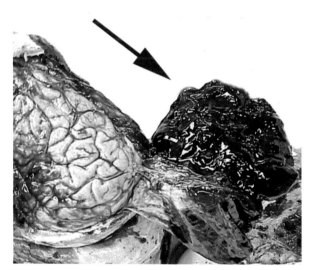

FIGURE 4.13 A closer view of the subdural hemorrhage. He also had a hypertensive bleed into his brainstem which caused him to fall and receive his other injuries.

FIGURE 4.14 An elderly woman was sexually assaulted and killed by multiple blows to the head. See next photo.

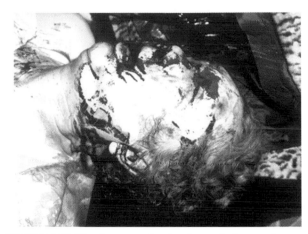

FIGURE 4.15 The damage to her head was obvious at the scene and in the autopsy room. See next photo.

FIGURE 4.16 A pattern was discovered on the decendent's face. See next photo.

FIGURE 4.17 The suspect was wearing a pair of these boots. See next photo.

FIGURE 4.18 The sole of the boot. See next photo.

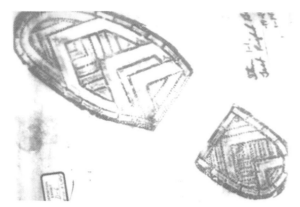

FIGURE 4.19 Fingerprint powder was placed over the sole and the pattern was copied onto a transparency. See next photo.

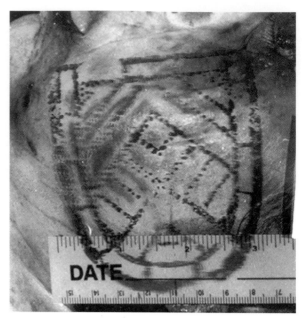

FIGURE 4.20 The transparency was placed over the face and the comparison was thought to be a match. The examiner could not prove with certainty the suspect's boot caused the injury; however, he could say with certainty that a boot with a similar sole made the mark.

FIGURE 4.21 An elderly woman was abducted and killed. She was buried for approximately ten days. See next photo.

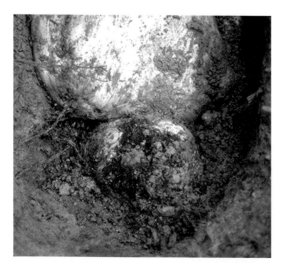

FIGURE 4.22 The body had not decomposed much at the time of its removal from the burial site. It was transferred to the morgue and placed in refrigeration. See next photo.

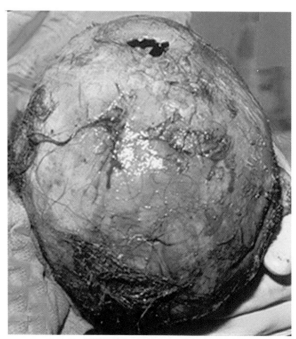

FIGURE 4.23 The autopsy was performed the next day. The body had significantly decomposed within the day after discovery. There were lacerations of the scalp and obvious fractures of the skull. See next photo.

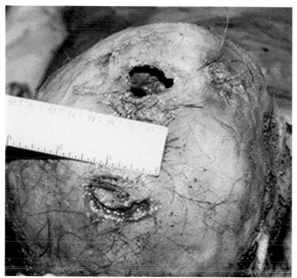

FIGURE 4.24 One of the lacerations had a semicircular pattern. See next photo.

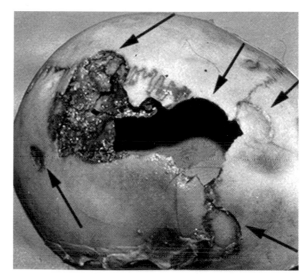

FIGURE 4.25 It was not until the skull was cleaned that the numerous semicircular patterns became evident. The woman had been struck numerous times with a hammer.

FIGURE 4.26 A triple homicide occurred at this convenience store after closing hours one night. The manager and two employees were killed. See next photo.

FIGURE 4.28 All of the bodies were discovered behind this door in the back. See next photo.

FIGURE 4.27 The cash register and safe had been opened. See next photo.

FIGURE 4.29 The man was in the cooler. He had been struck in the head multiple times, although law enforcement thought he and the others had been shot with shotguns because of the tremendous damage and amount of blood. See next photo.

FIGURE 4.30 The two women were in the bathroom. Both had been killed in that location. See next photo.

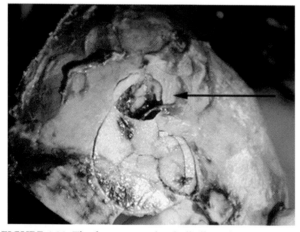

FIGURE 4.32 The fractures to the skull allowed an easier diagnosis to be made regarding the weapon. The depressed fracture was the typical circular pattern made by a hammer. See next photo.

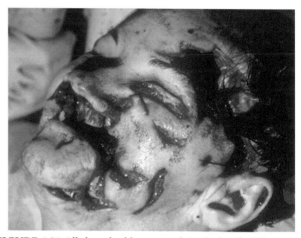

FIGURE 4.31 All three had been struck in the head with a hammer. The wounds were all on the left side as on this woman. See next photo.

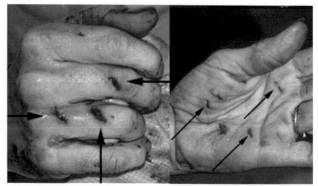

FIGURE 4.33 One of the women was stabbed in the hand with a screwdriver, in addition to being struck in the head.

FIGURE 4.34 This elderly woman was discovered dead in her kitchen. There were no signs of struggle in any other room; however, the house had been ransacked. See next photo.

FIGURE 4.35 A closer view of the body on the kitchen floor as she was discovered. See next photo.

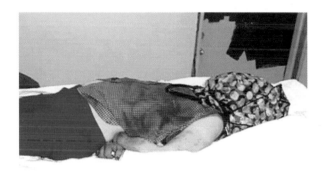

FIGURE 4.36 The body on the autopsy table. See next photo.

FIGURE 4.37 There was a bedspread wrapped around her head under the bag. See next photo.

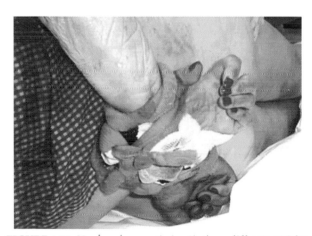

FIGURE 4.38 Her hands were tied with three different articles of clothing. See next photo.

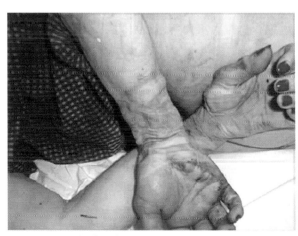

FIGURE 4.39 Her hands were swollen due to the constriction of the wrists by the ligatures. See next photo.

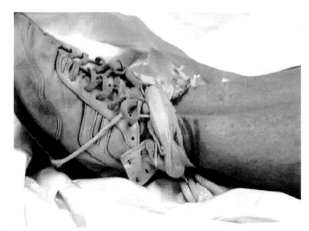

FIGURE 4.40 Her feet were bound together by a brassiere. See next photo.

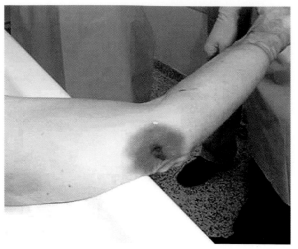

FIGURE 4.41 The injury to this elbow and one like it to the other elbow suggest the woman had her hands bound behind her when she was forced to the floor. See next photo.

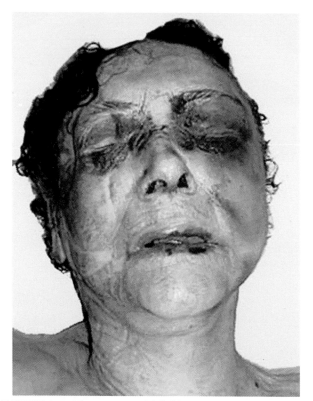

FIGURE 4.42 There were multiple blunt impacts to the face. See next photo.

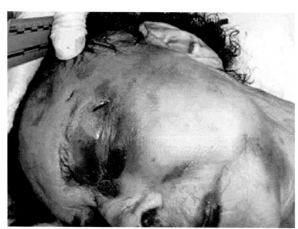

FIGURE 4.43 She was wearing glasses at the time she was struck. The laceration at the edge of the eye was caused by a blow to the glasses. See next photo.

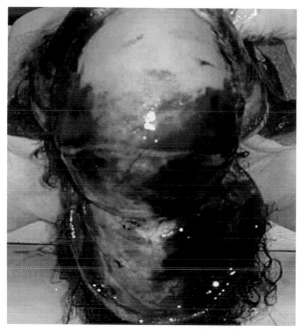

FIGURE 4.44 The degree of subscalpular hemorrhage illustrates the numerous impact injuries. She was not struck just a couple of times. See next photo.

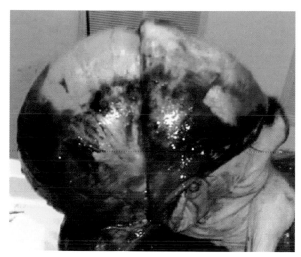

FIGURE 4.45 The subscalpular hemorrhages were more impressive on the right side. See next photo.

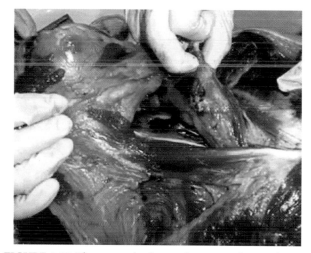

FIGURE 4.46 There was also hemorrhage over the vertebrae in the neck. See next photo.

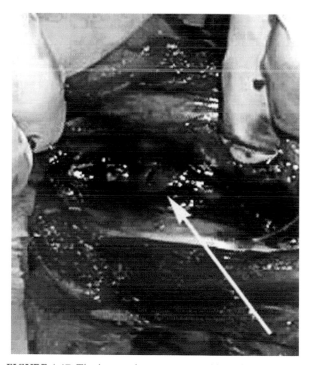

FIGURE 4.47 The hemorrhage was caused by a fracture of the neck (arrow). The fracture was caused by a violent hyperextension of the decedent's head.

Chapter 5

SUDDEN NATURAL DEATH

Most people believe the medical examiner or coroner deals only with traumatic deaths. In fact, most deaths reported to a medical examiner's office are due to natural causes. They are reported because most states required sudden and unexpected natural deaths to be investigated. The following are the most common diseases that cause sudden and unexpected death:

CARDIOVASCULAR DISEASE (HEART AND BLOOD VESSELS)

Atherosclerotic Cardiovascular Disease

Besides being the leading cause of death nationwide, atherosclerotic heart disease is also the leading cause of sudden unexpected natural death. Atherosclerosis ("hardening" of the arteries) refers to the fat and other deposits which build up on the inside lining of blood vessels. This can lead to a plugging of the vessel, preventing blood and oxygen from getting to the tissues. Atherosclerosis primarily affects the larger elastic arteries, such as the aorta, carotids, and iliacs, as well as smaller muscular arteries, such as the coronary arteries in the heart.

Atherosclerotic coronary artery disease is the most common cause of death due to heart disease. Proper oxygenation of the heart wall (myocardium) is prevented because of the plugging of the vessel. When severe, this buildup leads to chest pain, heart attacks, and arrhythmias (abnormal heart beats). Arrhythmias are the main complication of atherosclerotic coronary artery disease, causing sudden death. They cannot be detected by either gross or microscopic examination of the heart at autopsy because they are an electrical activity. Since it cannot be seen, an arrhythmia must be determined as the final event causing death by excluding all other possibilities. However, the atherosclerotic disease in the blood vessels is usually present at autopsy. Signs of heart attacks may or may not be evident. People die with varying amounts of disease and the amount of obstruction needed to cause death will vary between individuals and circumstances. A man with known severe triple vessel coronary artery disease may live for many years while one with only moderate single vessel disease may die suddenly without having any previous signs or symptoms.

Hypertensive Heart Disease (High Blood Pressure)

An enlarged heart with no other significant abnormalities except for generalized enlargement of the muscle walls is usually regarded as a hypertensive heart. In many instances, however, there will not be a history of high blood pressure. Sudden death in people with hypertensive heart disease may be due to an arrhythmia or one of the other complications of hypertensive cardiovascular disease, such as a rupture of the aorta or a hemorrhage in the brain.

Other Types of Heart Disease

Less common forms of heart disease which cause sudden death include congenital and valvular heart disease, cardiomyopathy, and myocarditis. There are numerous congenital abnormalities of the heart which may cause sudden death. Single coronary arteries and abnormal anatomic distributions of the coronaries are relatively common. Many severe congenital problems may be discovered at birth or shortly thereafter. Abnormalities of the heart valves, such as narrowings or ballooning (prolapse of the mitral valve) can cause sudden death. Cardiomyopathies or heart muscle disease, such as asymmetrical hypertrophy of the heart and dilated idiopathic cardiomyopathy, may cause sudden death at a young age, often during exercise. Sudden unexpected death from myocarditis (infection of the heart wall) may follow a flu-like illness.

Other Vascular Diseases (Blood Vessel Disease)

In addition to atherosclerotic disease, there are a number of vascular diseases which also cause sudden death. In most cases, death does not occur as rapidly as it does when there is a sudden cardiac arrhythmia. The following are some of the more common vascular diseases or disorders which cause sudden unexpected death.

1. *Ruptured cerebral aneurysm* — Aneurysms (a weakening and ballooning of a blood vessel) of the brain may rupture during a time of stress, a sudden increase in blood pressure, or during a nonstressful occasion. A ruptured vessel may be discovered at autopsy in an individual who has fallen and received other fatal injuries. In this unusual circumstance, the rupture precedes the fall and is not caused by the fall.

2. *Pulmonary thromboemboli* — The vast majority of emboli (blood clots which break away and travel from their site of origin) originate in the deep veins of the lower extremities. They most commonly develop in individuals who become bedridden after surgical procedures and in anyone whose activity level decreases suddenly. Sudden death occurs when large ones break away, travel through the heart, and plug up the blood vessels leading to the lungs.

3. *Ruptured aortic aneurysms* — Aneurysms of the aorta commonly occur in the abdomen where the aorta divides into the vessels that take blood to the legs. The aorta is especially prone to develop atherosclerosis and weakening of the vessel wall at this location. Most of these aneurysms are diagnosed prior to rupture and can be dealt with surgically. Unfortunately, some rupture unexpectedly and death usually happens quickly.

4. *Acute aortic dissection* — Acute aortic dissection is associated with high blood pressure and other uncommon disorders. The aortic wall splits apart, causing considerable pain and death unless the dissection occurs close to or in a hospital where care can be provided immediately. Aortic dissections are also seen in cocaine and methamphetamine abusers.

RESPIRATORY (BREATHING AND LUNG) DISORDERS

Sudden and unexpected deaths from respiratory disorders are usually due to infections. Infants and the elderly may succumb to pneumonia very suddenly and without exhibiting significant symptoms. Viral infections of the airway may become secondarily infected by bacteria. An immunocompromised individual with AIDS or cancer readily develops respiratory infections, but these deaths are usually chronic and expected. Rarely, undiagnosed tuberculosis and other contagious diseases not associated with an immunocompromised host still cause unexpected deaths.

BRAIN AND SPINAL CORD (CENTRAL NERVOUS SYSTEM)

There are a few disorders of the central nervous system (CNS) that cause sudden and unexpected death. For example, brain tumors can cause sudden death, but people with tumors usually present to a physician with evidence of their disease prior to death. Occasionally, someone may die suddenly from an unsuspected and undiagnosed rapidly growing tumor. Colloid cysts of the third ventricle may also cause a sudden unexpected death. Meningitis may present with nonspecific symptoms such as a headache and may not be diagnosed in an ER, but within hours the symptoms may progress rapidly and cause death before adequate medical attention is obtained.

The most common disorder of the CNS that causes a sudden death is a seizure. Seizures may be idiopathic (unknown cause) or acquired. If the decedent developed a seizure disorder as a result of blunt trauma to the head, death is not considered natural because the cause of death was the result of the trauma. Examples of acquired seizures from natural causes are accidents and tumors. It is important to recognize that the correct cause of death is the underlying disorder, not the seizure. Finally, there is a group of patients with seizures who have no underlying cause. In these deaths the cause of death may be ruled "idiopathic seizure disorder." The identification at autopsy of either a gross or microscopic abnormality in the brain that triggers the seizure is rarely found. Like cardiac arrhythmias, seizures are electrical activity which is not in itself detectable during the autopsy. Clearly, the decedent's history and the elimination of other causes of death are important when making the proper diagnosis.

CHRONIC ALCOHOLISM

Chronic alcoholics usually die from medical complications which are easily diagnosable; however, they can die suddenly from no apparent cause. In such cases, there is usually little disease seen at autopsy. The decedent's heart may be slightly enlarged and weak due to the toxic effects of alcohol, or there may be no discernable cardiac abnormality. Deaths due to chronic alcoholism are considered natural, while deaths from acute alcohol intoxication are considered accidental.

UNDETERMINED NATURAL CAUSES

At least 1–2% of the deaths in a busy forensic jurisdiction will be undetermined and a majority of those will be due to natural causes. The autopsy will be negative. The pathologist will be unable to find a cause of death after a complete autopsy that includes microscopic and toxicological studies. Such decedents tend to be younger individuals who have had no previous injuries or medical problems. The mechanism of death in these cases must be an arrhythmia of the heart; however, the cause cannot be determined.

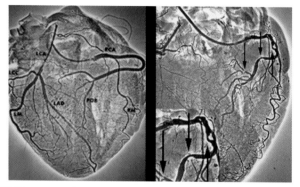

FIGURE 5.1 These are hearts that have been injected with dye postmortem. The heart on the left has normal undamaged coronary arteries. The heart on the right has narrowed blood vessels (arrows) due to atherosclerosis (hardening of the arteries).

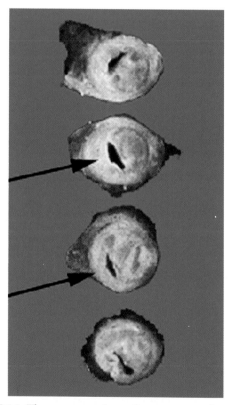

FIGURE 5.2 These cross-sections of coronary arteries are plugged with atherosclerotic disease (hardening of the arteries). The arrows point to the only openings (dark areas) in the vessels. The yellow material is the atherosclerosis.

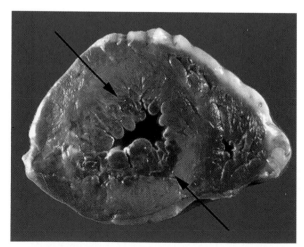

FIGURE 5.3 The earliest noticeable signs of a heart attack is dark colored muscle (arrows). This discoloration reveals the heart attack to be hours old at the time of death.

FIGURE 5.4 This heart shows the yellow discoloration of a heart attack which is approximately a week old (arrows).

FIGURE 5.5 This is the inside of the left ventricular heart wall showing the white scarring from an old heart attack.

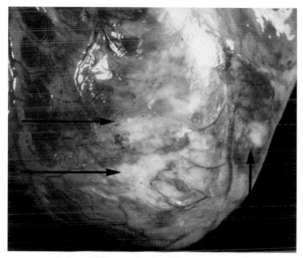

FIGURE 5.6 An old heart attack will appear as a white scar on the outside of the heart wall (arrows).

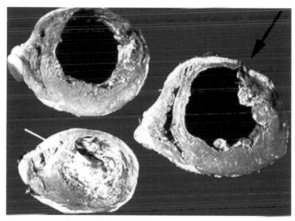

FIGURE 5.7 The complications of heart attacks include a rupture of the heart wall (black arrow) and the formation of a blood clot (white arrow).

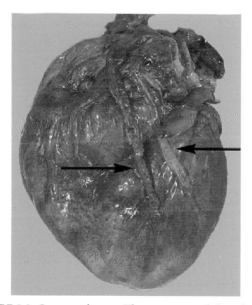

FIGURE 5.8 Coronary bypass. The arrows reveal the veins that have been used to jump across the plugged coronary arteries. The veins usually come from the legs.

FIGURE 5.9 This man was discovered in a recreation center. His position suggests a sudden collapse and death. See next photo.

FIGURE 5.10 His clothes had been removed and neatly placed on the bench. See next photo.

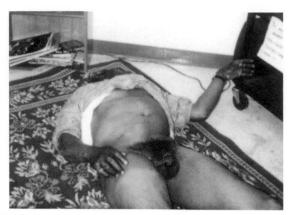

FIGURE 5.11 He was wearing a condom. The woman he had been with later confessed he had collapsed suddenly prior to having sex. An autopsy revealed significant coronary artery disease and numerous old heart attacks.

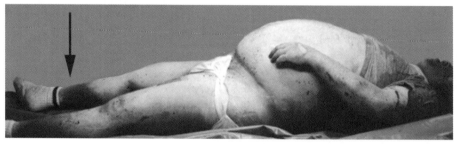

FIGURE 5.12 This obese man died suddenly. The arrow points to the dark and thickened skin of the lower legs, which is a sign of poor circulation and heart disease.

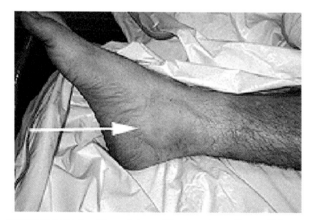

FIGURE 5.13 Swelling of the ankles is a sign of heart failure. See next photo.

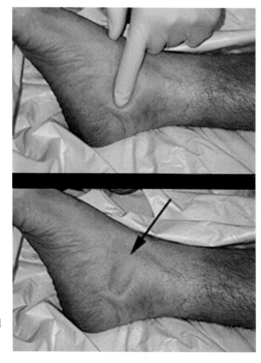

FIGURE 5.14 An indentation remaining on the skin after pressure is called "pitting edema." This edema is another sign the heart is failing.

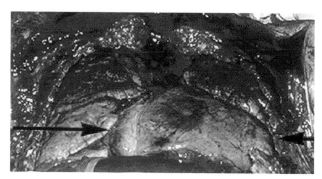

FIGURE 5.15 An enlarged heart is a sign of chronic heart failure. This heart (between the arrows) is more than twice the size of normal. See next photo.

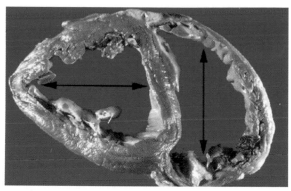

FIGURE 5.16 A cross-section of the heart in the previous photo would look like this. The chambers are dilated and the walls are thinner than normal.

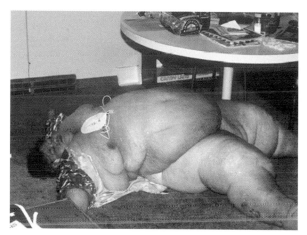

FIGURE 5.17 Obese individuals have enlarged hearts and are prone to die suddenly. See next photo.

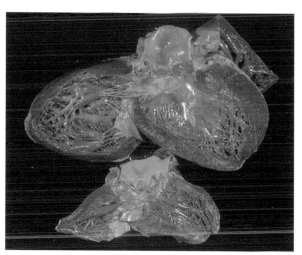

FIGURE 5.18 An enlarged heart from obesity or high blood pressure (top) may be twice the size of normal (bottom).

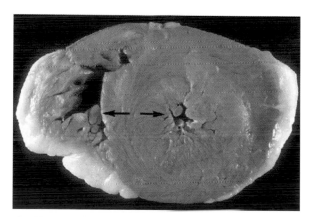

FIGURE 5.19 The wall (arrows) in this cross-section is very thick. This is a sign of hypertension (high blood pressure).

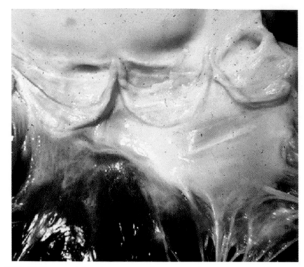

FIGURE 5.20 This is a normal aortic valve. See next photo.

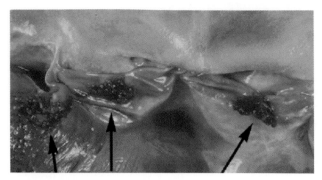

FIGURE 5.21 This aortic valve has vegetations of bacteria (arrows) from possible chronic drug abuse. Compare with previous photo.

FIGURE 5.22 Normal mitral valve. See next photo.

FIGURE 5.23 Abnormal mitral valve with thickened leaflets. This is a "ballooning" mitral valve which caused sudden death. Compare with previous photo.

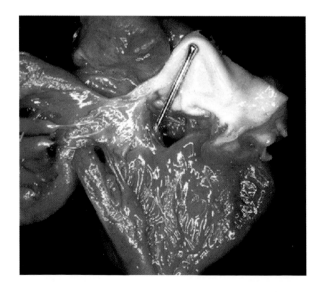

FIGURE 5.24 The metal probe is sticking through a ventricular septal defect (opening) which is a congenital abnormality which can cause sudden death.

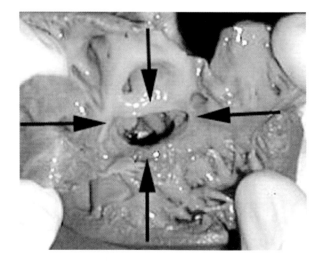

FIGURE 5.25 This is another septal defect in a three-week-old child who occasionally stopped breathing and would turn blue. The defect was not detected at birth or upon regular check-ups.

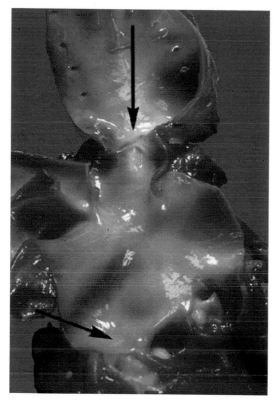

FIGURE 5.26 The aortic arch in this child was congenitally narrowed. The upper arrow shows the constriction. The lower arrow points to the aortic valve.

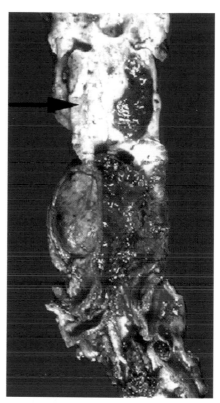

FIGURE 5.27 This is the lower part of the aorta which shows advanced atherosclerotic disease. A normal aorta should be thin and yellow (arrow). This aorta is thickened and has so much wall damage it is prone to rupture.

FIGURE 5.28 This aorta ruptured into the bowel and caused sudden death by bleeding. The initial body examination might show bleeding from the rectum

FIGURE 5.29 This lady's left leg is more swollen than the right. Blood clots in the legs will cause them to swell. A blood clot can break loose, travel through the heart, and plug up the blood vessels in the lungs. See next photo.

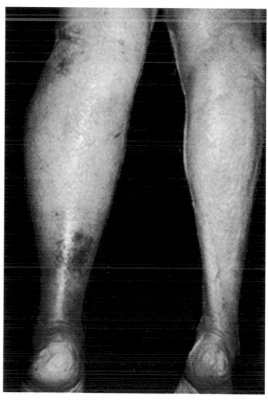

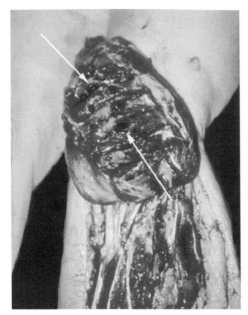

FIGURE 5.30 This swollen leg was opened to reveal the dark blood clots (thrombi) in the calf muscle vessels (arrows).

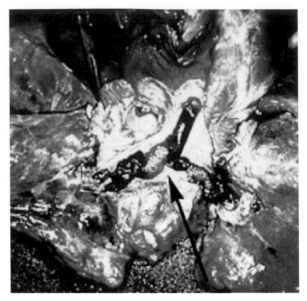

FIGURE 5.31 Pulmonary thromboemboli. Blood clots (arrow) have broken away from the legs and traveled up the body to lodge in the large blood vessels of the lungs. This caused chest pain and sudden death.

FIGURE 5.32 This lung has abundant black pigment (anthracosis) on its surface. The person with this lung either smoked or worked in a coal mine.

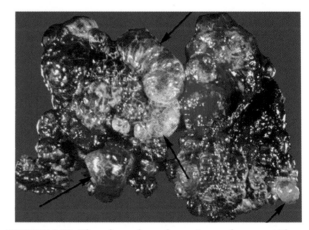

FIGURE 5.33 These lungs have dramatic emphysema with balloon-type expansions on their surfaces (arrows). This means the lung tissue has been destroyed (usually from smoking) and the person has difficulty getting oxygen into the lungs.

FIGURE 5.34 This lung has smaller holes than the previous case. This sponge-like appearance is also typical for advanced chronic emphysema.

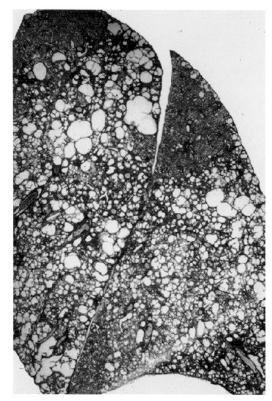

FIGURE 5.35 Another presentation of emphysema showing the holes in the lungs caused by smoking. This change causes the right side of the heart to thicken which renders it prone to failure.

FIGURE 5.36 This lung has firm white areas (arrows) of pneumonia.

FIGURE 5.37 Sudden death in the bathtub. He ruptured a cerebral (brain) aneurysm.

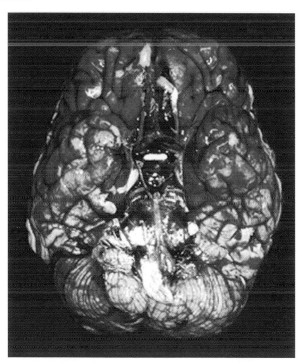

FIGURE 5.38 Ruptured cerebral aneurysm. A ballooned blood vessel ruptured over the bottom of this brain. This caused a marked hemorrhage (subarachnoid) over the base, sides, and top of the brain.

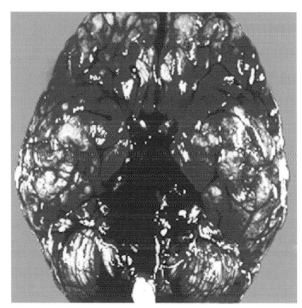

FIGURE 5.39 Another case of marked subarachnoid hemorrhage originating over the base of the brain. Most of these hemorrhages occur naturally from ruptured aneurysms; however, some can be caused by minor trauma or rupture secondary to drugs such as cocaine and methamphetamine.

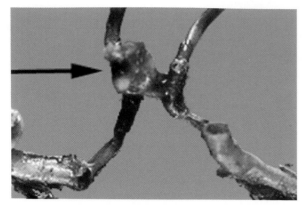

FIGURE 5.40 This is an aneurysm (ballooned-out blood vessel) which was located on the base of the brain. It ruptured and caused death.

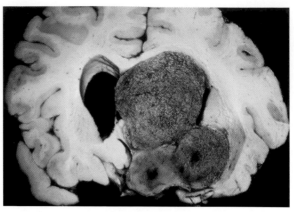

FIGURE 5.41 The darker masses are cancer of the brain. Brain cancer rarely causes sudden unexpected death, but it may.

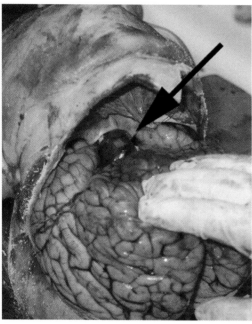

FIGURE 5.42 This area of swelling at the base of the brain was the finding in the sudden death of an eight year old. He complained of a headache the night he died. See next photo.

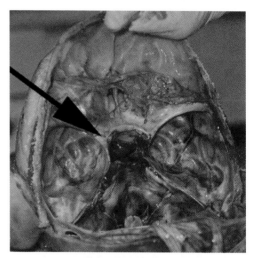

FIGURE 5.43 The pituitary gland rests in this area at the base of the skull. This area is much more expanded than usual due to the growth of a tumor. See next photo.

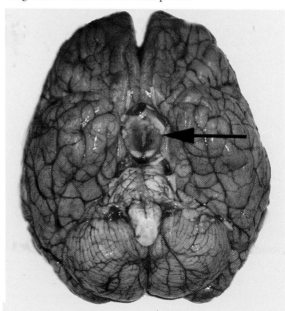

FIGURE 5.44 This photo of the base of the brain shows the area of the tumor.

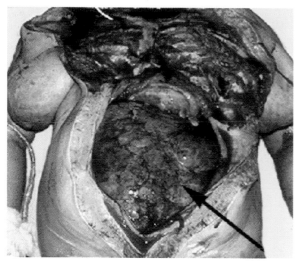

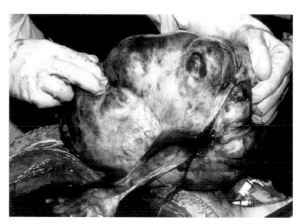

FIGURE 5.46 The tumor was of ovarian origin and it weighed 26 lbs.

FIGURE 5.45 This lady came into the emergency room and died within a few hours. No one knew she had a huge tumor in her abdomen. See next photo.

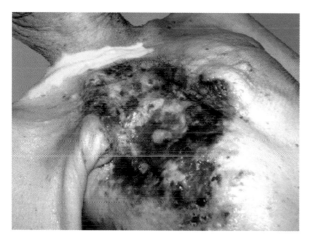

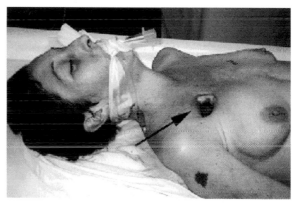

FIGURE 5.48 This woman had received treatment for cancer of the lung. There was a hole in her chest wall (arrow) through which the lung could be seen. She died of infection.

FIGURE 5.47 This is cancer of the breast after treatment. The woman died at home. The cancer had spread (metastasized) throughout her body. Breast cancer is rarely a cause of sudden and unexpected death.

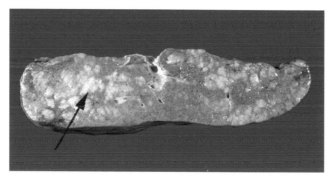

FIGURE 5.49 Metastatic cancer to the liver. The white nodules are the cancer.

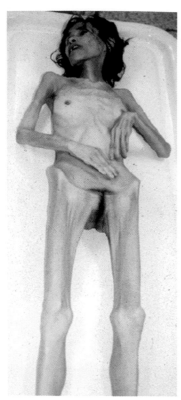

FIGURE 5.50 Marked emaciation. This woman died of starvation.

FIGURE 5.51 This man collapsed in the bathroom. There was blood on the toilet and the floor. See next photo.

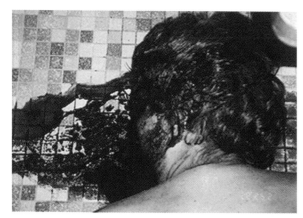

FIGURE 5.52 All of the blood on the floor came from his mouth. He was an alcoholic who had a damaged liver (cirrhosis) which caused blood vessels in the esophagus to become thickened. These thickened vessels (varices) are prone to rupture, as in this case. He bled to death.

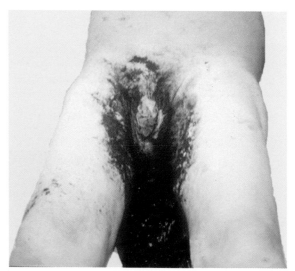

FIGURE 5.53 Chronic alcoholics can also bleed from varices in the rectum.

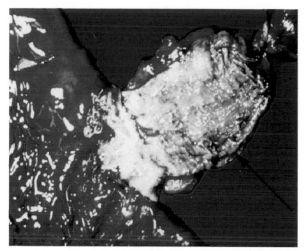

FIGURE 5.55 This liver has cirrhosis (scars) from both alcohol and hepatitis.

FIGURE 5.54 This is the distal esophagus in a chronic alcoholic. The arrow points to the thickened varices. The stomach (to the left) is red because of irritation from the alcohol.

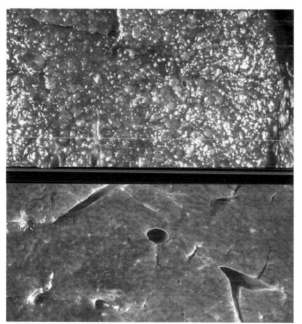

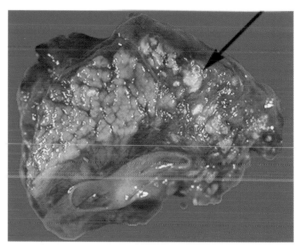

FIGURE 5.57 Alcoholics can also have inflammation to the pancreas (pancreatitis). The arrow points to the yellow area of inflammation.

FIGURE 5.56 This illustrates the difference between a cirrhotic liver from alcohol abuse (upper) and a normal liver (lower).

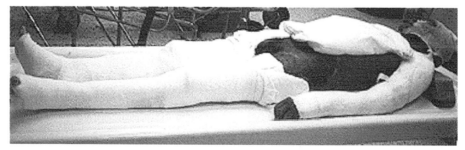

FIGURE 5.58 This African-American man developed a severe reaction to antibiotics. This type of injury should not be confused with thermal injury. See next photo.

FIGURE 5.59 The outer layer of his skin slipped off most of his body. Some of the skin (arrow) on his chest became mummified while he was alive. See next photo.

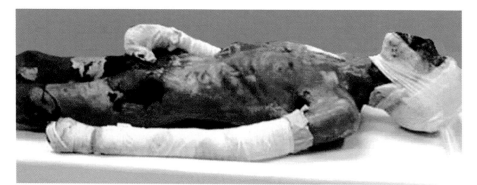

FIGURE 5.60 A closer view of the extent of the damage and the mummification to the chest. See next photo.

FIGURE 5.61 The lower extremities were also affected. See next photo.

FIGURE 5.62 Another case of skin slippage from a reaction to antibiotics. A view of his back reveals the extent of the injury to this African-American man. This change should not be confused with thermal injury.

Chapter 6

FIREARMS (HANDGUNS AND RIFLES)

Handguns and rifles fire ammunition or cartridges composed of a primer, gunpowder or propellant, and a bullet or projectile. When the firing pin of a weapon strikes the primer, the resulting explosion ignites the gunpowder. Gunpowder, vaporized primer, and metal from a gun may be deposited on skin and/or clothing of the victim. The presence and location of primer elements on the hands help to indicate who may have fired the weapon in question.

Gunpowder comes out of the muzzle in two forms.

1. Completely burned gunpowder, called "soot" or "fouling," can be washed off the skin.
2. Particles of burning and unburned powder can become embedded in the skin or bounce off and abrade the skin. The marks on the skin are called "tattooing" or "stippling."

The presence or absence of gunpowder on the clothing or skin indicates whether the gunshot was contact (loose or tight), close, intermediate, or distant.

Tight contact — All gunpowder residue is on the edges or in the depths of a wound. There may be searing or burning of wound margins, or reddening of surrounding skin due to carbon monoxide gas produced by burning powder. There is often tearing of the skin around the entrance wound (especially in head wounds) because of pressure buildup and blow-back of the skin toward the muzzle.

Loose contact — Gunpowder may escape from the barrel and be deposited around the edges of a wound.

Close range — Close range gunshot wounds occur at muzzle-to-target distances of approximately 6–12". Both fouling and stippling are present.

Intermediate range — These wounds occur at muzzle-to-target distances of approximately 12" to 3'. There is no fouling, only stippling or deposition of particles on clothing.

Distant wounds — No fouling or stippling.

The amount of gunpowder emanating from the muzzle is different among weapons and the same weapon with different ammunition. A particular gun in question must be test-fired with the same ammunition if accurate comparisons are to be made.

Entrance and exit wounds are generally easy to differentiate. Entrance wounds tend to be circular defects with a thin rim of abrasion caused by a bullet scraping and perforating the skin. Entrance wounds of the face can be quite atypical appearing because the surfaces are not flat.

Exit wounds may be circular like entrance wounds, but they are more often irregular in shape. They may be slit-like or have ragged edges. They do not have a rim of abrasion like entrance wounds unless a victim's skin is pressed against another object. This is called a "shored" exit wound. Skin around an exit wound may also be discolored because of underlying bleeding in the soft tissues.

The scene must be examined for bullets and cartridges. Bullets may be under the body or caught in clothing after exiting the body.

FIGURE 6.1 Firearms take many lives each year. All information from both the scene and the wounds must be gathered in order to determine both the cause and manner of death. This man appears to have committed suicide. His gun was next to him on the couch. The wound (arrow) must be examined and investigation needs to take place in order to determine if his death is consistent with suicide.

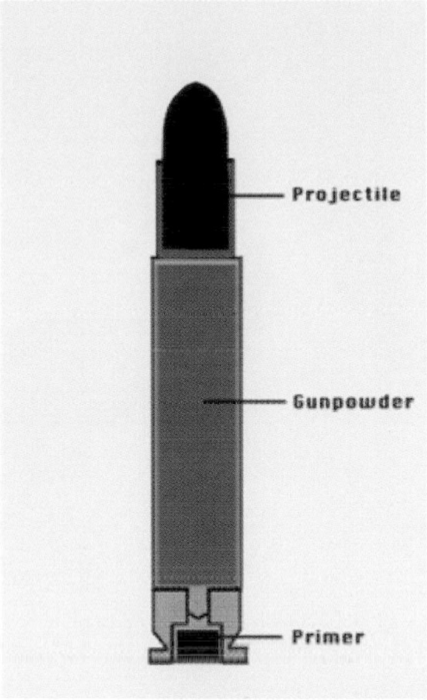

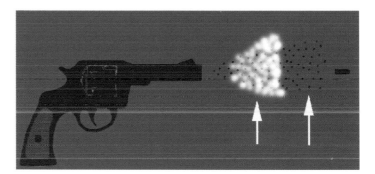

FIGURE 6.2 The cartridge used in guns and rifles have a projectile, gunpowder, and the primer which ignites when the firing pin strikes the base of the cartridge. A gunpowder residue test checks for the presence of primer.

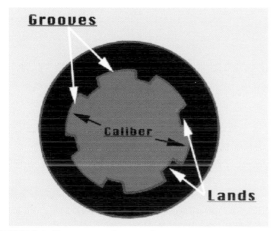

FIGURE 6.3 "Lands and Grooves" on the inside of handguns and rifles give the bullet a better trajectory. All bullets fired from the same gun can be matched to each other and to the gun because of these markings.

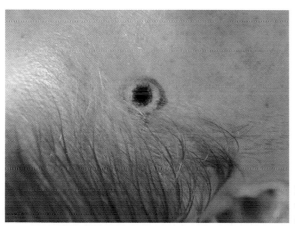

FIGURE 6.4 Gunpowder exits the muzzle in two forms. 1) completely burned powder (soot or fouling) and 2) burning and unburned particles (stippling or tattooing). The particles will travel further than the soot and will abrade the skin.

FIGURE 6.5 This is a typical low velocity tight contact gunshot wound to the head. The gunpowder is in the depths of the wound and there is a muzzle abrasion around the central defect.

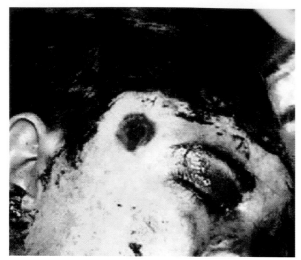

FIGURE 6.6 Tight contact gunshot wound. There is more skin abrasion around the wound than in the previous case. All of the powder is in the wound.

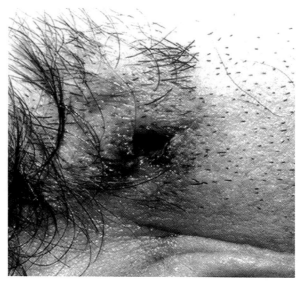

FIGURE 6.7 The bright red discoloration around the entrance of this contact wound is due to carbon monoxide in the tissues.

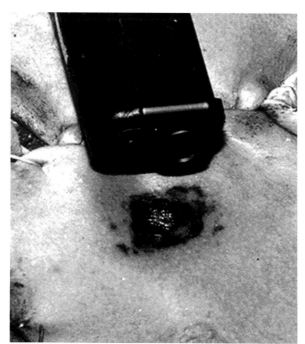

FIGURE 6.8 The wound on the chest matches the muzzle of the gun.

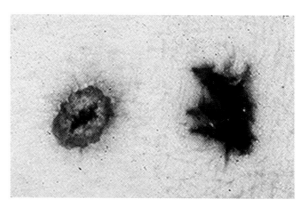

FIGURE 6.9 The wound on the left is a typical distant wound and the wound on the left is the exit. Not all exit wounds are irregularly shaped and larger than the entrance wound.

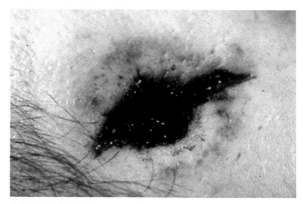

FIGURE 6.10 Contact wound of entrance with powder on the edges and slight splitting of the skin. Skin splits are common in contact wounds of the head; the skin is forced back because of the pressure buildup occurring between the skin and the bone of the skull.

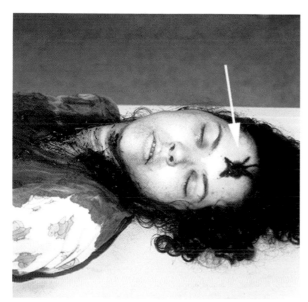

FIGURE 6.11 Women do shoot themselves in the head. See next photo.

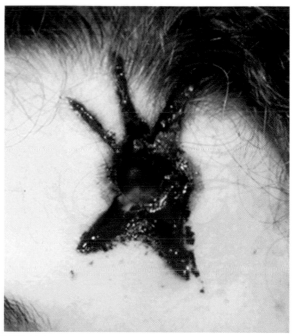

FIGURE 6.12 There are extensive lacerations around the wound. This is typical of a large caliber bullet. Notice the powder around the edges.

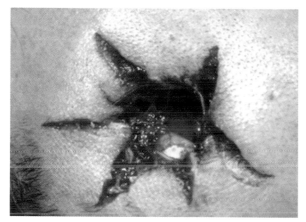

FIGURE 6.13 This is a very explosive contact wound of the skull from a large caliber gun. All of the powder is in the depths of the wound.

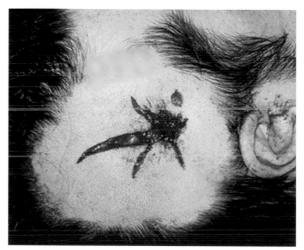

FIGURE 6.14 This contact wound of entrance with lacerations is larger than the exit wound. See next photo.

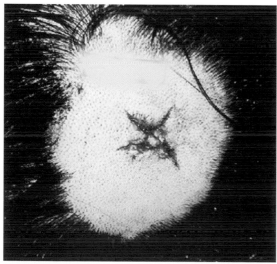

FIGURE 6.15 The exit wound is smaller than the entrance wound.

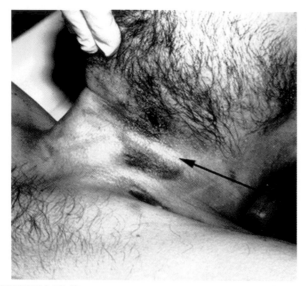

FIGURE 6.16 This loose contact wound has a pale area (arrow) where the skin fold of the neck blocked out the powder.

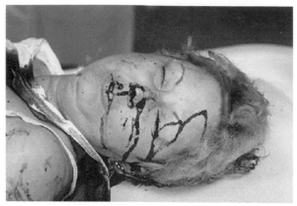

FIGURE 6.17 This woman died of a gunshot wound; however, no entrance site was seen. See next photo.

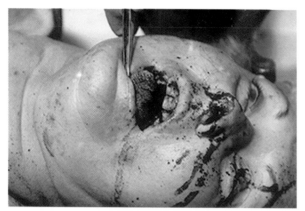

FIGURE 6.18 Opening her mouth reveals the powder from an intraoral gunshot wound.

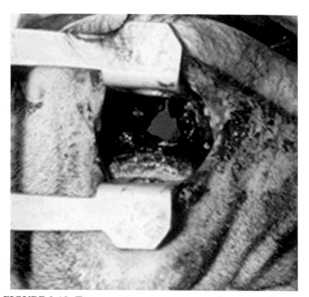

FIGURE 6.19 This was the previous woman's partner. They shot themselves in the mouth rather than be taken into custody. The black pigment is obvious on the tongue and on the roof of the mouth.

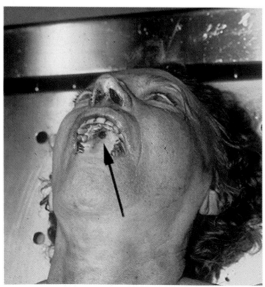

FIGURE 6.20 This is a contact gunshot wound of the mouth.

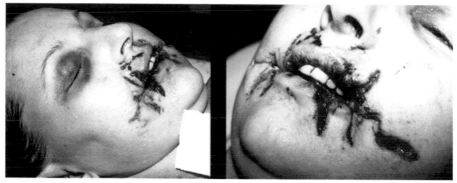

FIGURE 6.21 Splits of the skin around the mouth may occur in intraoral gunshot wounds. Notice the spectacle hemorrhages from skull fractures caused by the gunshot wound.

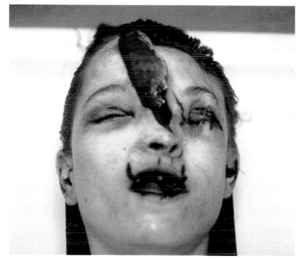

FIGURE 6.22 This intraoral gunshot wound caused enough pressure buildup in the cranial cavity to fracture the skull and lacerate the skin of the head. The large laceration is not the exit wound.

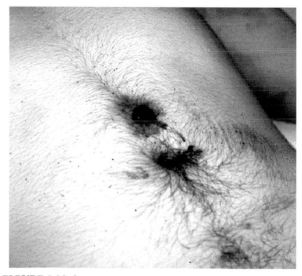

FIGURE 6.23 Loose contact gunshot wound of the abdomen. Suicide.

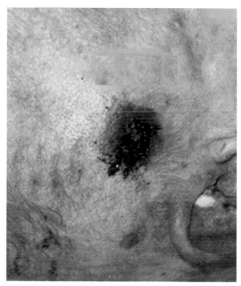

FIGURE 6.24 This gunshot wound to the head has abundant soot around the wound. The wound is then washed to check for stippling. See next photo.

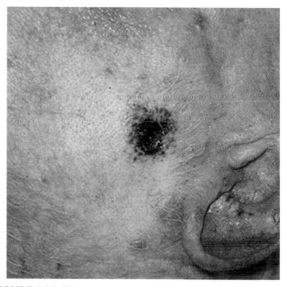

FIGURE 6.25 The wound has been washed and there is stippling. This indicates a close range gunshot wound because both stippling and fouling are present.

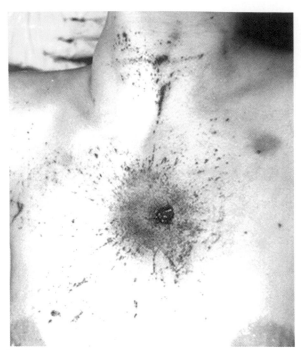

FIGURE 6.27 This is the shirt the woman was wearing when she shot herself. A distant shot would not have caused such a large hole.

FIGURE 6.26 This is an unusual close range suicide gunshot wound to the chest. The woman was wearing a T-shirt. See next photo.

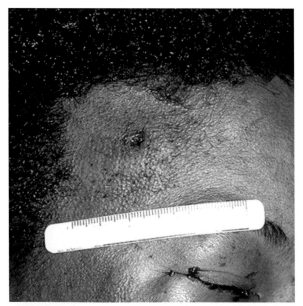

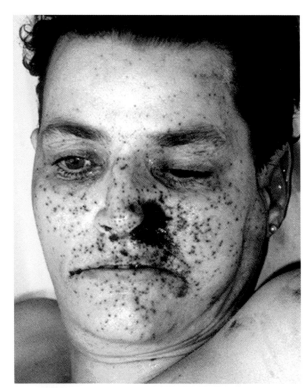

FIGURE 6.28 The gunshot wound on this forehead had both stippling and fouling. This indicates the gun was fired from less than a foot away from the victim.

FIGURE 6.29 This is an example of an intermediate wound with stippling and no fouling. The weapon was between 1–3 feet away from the victim when it was fired.

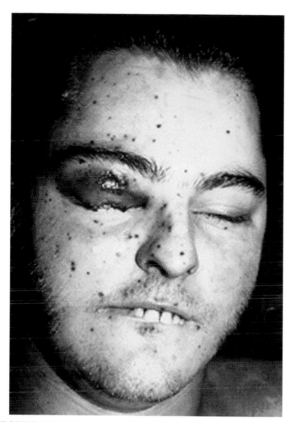

FIGURE 6.30 The man died from an intermediate gunshot wound. There was no fouling, only stippling. The main defect is in the middle of the eyelid while the edge of the eyelid was damaged at the same time. This indicates the man was shot while his eye was open.

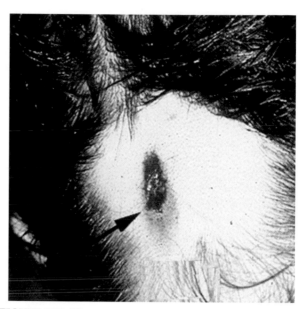

FIGURE 6.31 This wound to the back of the head has an abrasion on the superior aspect. The bullet scraped the skin as it entered the neck. The bullet was discovered in the chest.

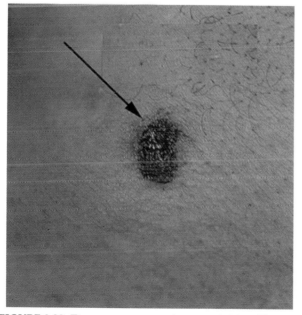

FIGURE 6.32 The arrow points to the central defect. There is no gunpowder. The skin is abraded below the entrance site, indicating the direction of the bullet toward the top of the photo.

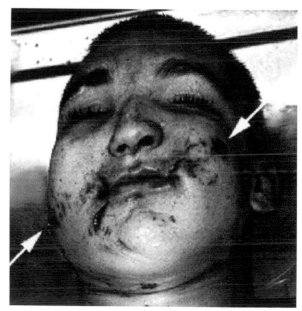

FIGURE 6.33 This is a gunshot wound through the mouth. The pressure caused splits of the skin around the mouth.

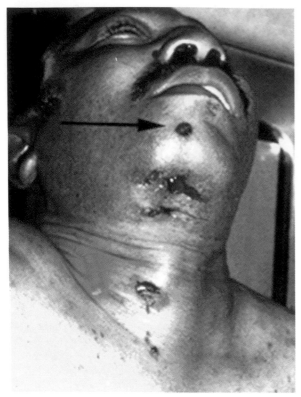

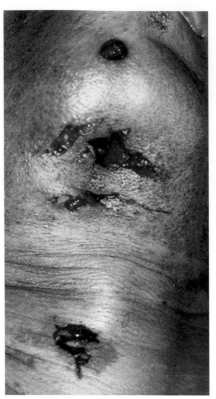

FIGURE 6.34 This man was shot as he was climbing the stairs to his home. A distant entrance wound is in the chin (arrow). See next photo.

FIGURE 6.35 The bullet exited under the chin and reentered the neck. See next photo.

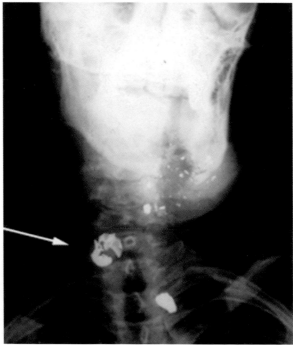

FIGURE 6.36 An X-ray of the neck shows two separate large opaque objects. The arrow points toward the jacket of the bullet. This is the most important object to recover because it has the rifling markings from the gun.

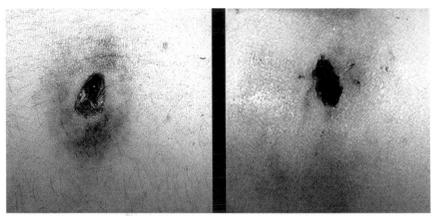

FIGURE 6.37 These are fairly typical exit wounds with hemorrhage in the tissues around the central defect. However, an entrance wound may have a similar appearance.

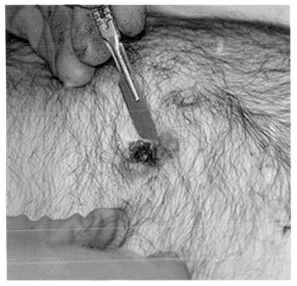

FIGURE 6.38 Bullets expend energy perforating the skin. It is not unusual to find the bullet just under the skin after it has passed through the body.

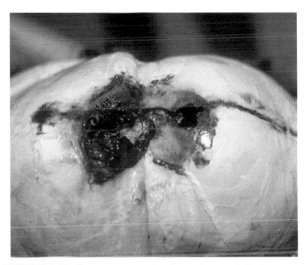

FIGURE 6.39 Gunpowder under the scalp may help determine the distance if no powder is seen externally. This is a contact wound.

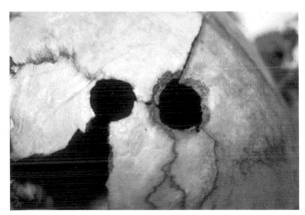

FIGURE 6.40 The skull is made up of two plates of bone. When a bullet enters the skull a "beveled" defect will occur on the opposite side of the bone. In this photo there is an entrance on the left and an exit on the right.

FIGURE 6.41 There is a gunshot wound of the skull in these skeletal remains. Notice the beveling on the inside of the skull, proving this to be an entrance wound.

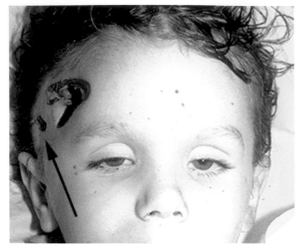

FIGURE 6.42 This child was shot in the head by a sibling. Sometimes wounds do not have the typical appearance if they enter the body over angled surfaces. See next photo.

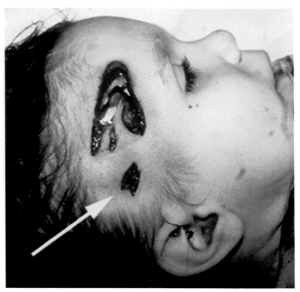

FIGURE 6.43 The arrow points to the exit wound which is much smaller than the entrance wound.

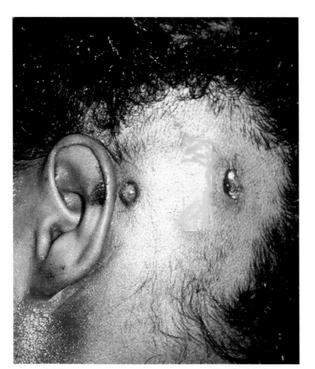

FIGURE 6.44 This woman died from a bone fragment which penetrated the brain. The bullet entered the ear and scalp and then ricocheted off the skull and out the scalp.

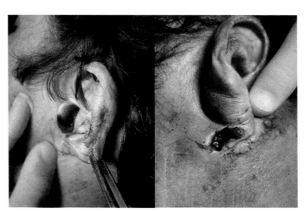

FIGURE 6.45 The photographs show the entrance (left) and the exit (right) of a gunshot wound to the head. The bullet passed through the head behind the jaw, but it did not enter the skull or directly damage the spinal cord. The woman died from damage to the spinal cord by the shock of the bullet as it passed through the head.

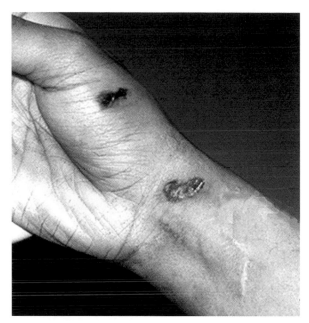

FIGURE 6.46 These are graze wounds from bullets.

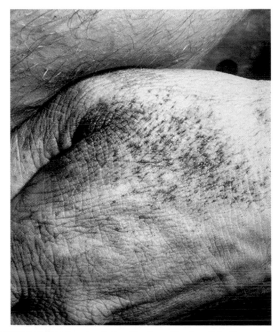

FIGURE 6.47 Powder (stippling) on the hand indicates the position of the hand at the time the gun was fired.

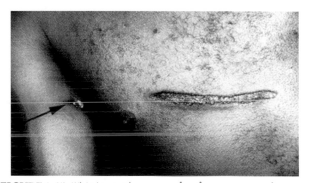

FIGURE 6.48 This is another example of a graze wound or a "gutter" wound. The bullet passed through the soft tissues of the chest before it entered the arm.

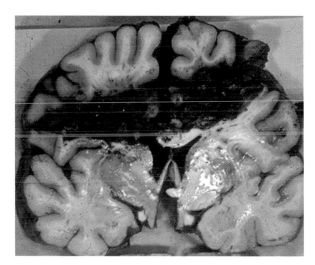

FIGURE 6.49 A gunshot to the head causes a marked expansion of the brain material as the bullet travels through the brain.

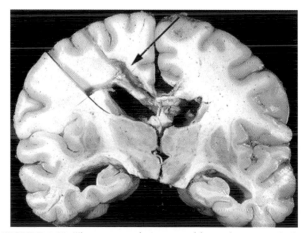

FIGURE 6.50 The arrow points to an old gunshot wound of the brain.

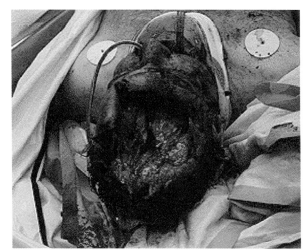

FIGURE 6.52 The result of a contact high velocity rifle shot to the head in this suicide. Powder may be difficult to find, but it should be present at the entrance site.

FIGURE 6.51 A man was shot in the chest and the bullet traveled through the liver (lower) and then through the heart (upper).

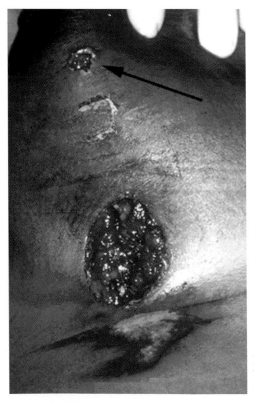

FIGURE 6.53 Marked destruction of the head from an intraoral shot (suicide). Notice the EKG patches, neck brace, and tubes in the mouth from resuscitation attempts.

FIGURE 6.54 The arrow points to the entrance wound in this woman's breast. She was shot with a rifle. The bullet went through the breast and reentered the body, making the larger defect.

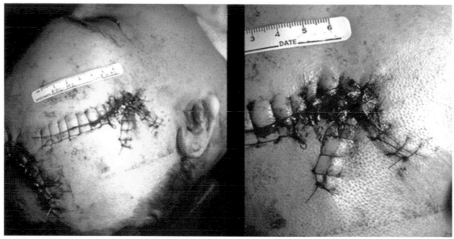

FIGURE 6.55 The examiner may have to look at cases after physicians have attempted therapy. Here, an entrance site from a rifle wound has been removed by the surgeon. The wounds have been distorted by the therapy. See next photo.

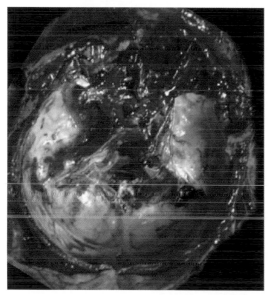

FIGURE 6.56 This view of the inside of a skull after the brain was removed shows the massive destruction from a high velocity rifle shot in this suicide.

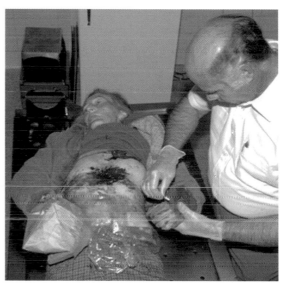

FIGURE 6.57 This officer is performing a gunshot residue test looking for the presence or absence of primer material on the decedent's hands.

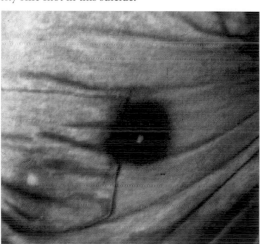

FIGURE 6.58 The gunpowder on this shirt proves the distance was within a couple of feet or less. There may have been little or no gunpowder on the skin around the entrance site.

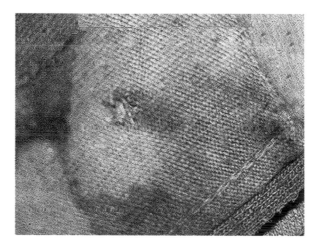

FIGURE 6.59 This discoloration on the collar around the hole is grease wiped off from the bullet. It is not from gunpowder.

Chapter 7

FIREARMS CASES

FIGURE 7.1 A man was discovered seated at his dining table. He committed suicide by shooting himself in the head. See next photo.

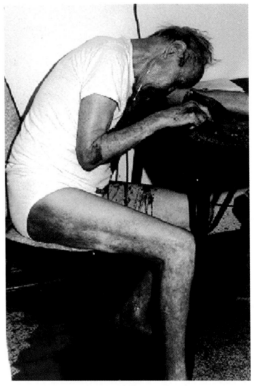

FIGURE 7.2 He was still seated after the injury. Blood had pooled onto the floor. See next photo.

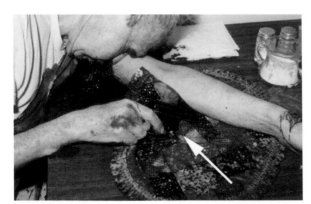

FIGURE 7.3 The gun is still in his hand (arrow). See next photo.

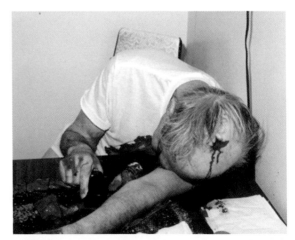

FIGURE 7.4 A different view of the gun in his hand and the obvious exit wound to the top of his head. The entrance wound in the mouth could not be examined at the scene. See next photo.

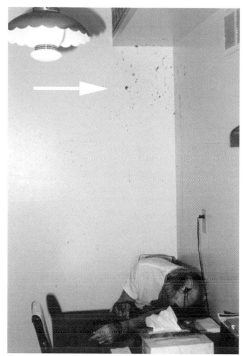

FIGURE 7.5 The arrow points to the bullet hole. There are also blood spatters to the right of the hole. These findings give the examiner the position of the body at the time the gun was fired.

FIGURE 7.8 A bullet hole in her glasses shows how she was shot in the right eye. See next photo.

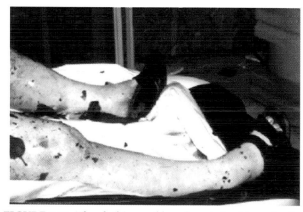

FIGURE 7.10 The clothing and her shoes helped to make the identification. See next photo.

FIGURE 7.6 These decomposed remains are of a woman who was shot in the head. She had recently given birth to a child she planned to sell. When she decided not to sell the child, she was murdered. See next photo.

FIGURE 7.7 There is a gunshot wound of exit on the back of the head. See next photo.

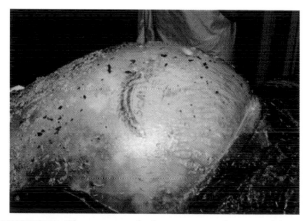

FIGURE 7.9 There was marked postmortem decomposition consistent with the five days she was missing in the summertime. See next photo.

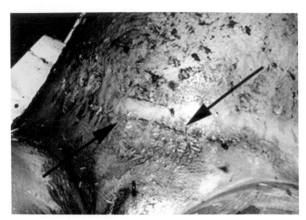

FIGURE 7.11 Her recently sutured cesarean incision was pulling apart because of the bloating. This also helped to make the identification. The assailant confessed to killing the woman.

FIGURE 7.12 This woman was shot in the arm by an estranged boyfriend. The photograph was taken during the resuscitation attempt. See next photo.

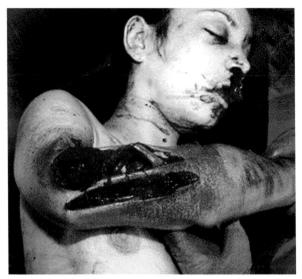

FIGURE 7.13 She was shot with a .357. There is stippling on the arm in addition to the markedly destroyed arm. There is also a wound to the face. See next photo.

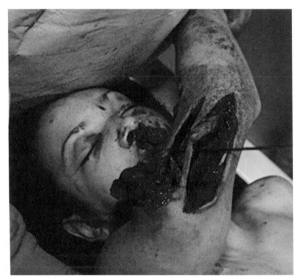

FIGURE 7.14 The arm is positioned in front of the face to show how one shot could account for all the injuries. See next photo.

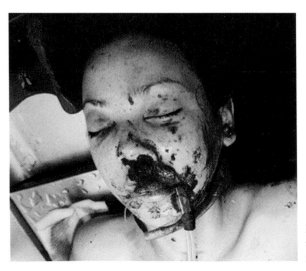

FIGURE 7.15 The facial wounds consisted of a gunshot wound below the nose and other injuries from the bone fragments of the arm. See next photo.

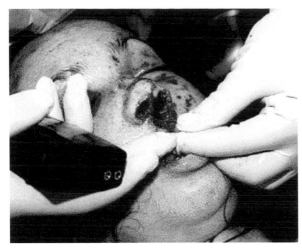

FIGURE 7.16 The edges of the injury to the face can be approximated to show it was caused by a gunshot wound. See next photo.

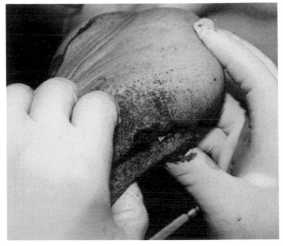

FIGURE 7.17 The injuries to the arm can be approximated to show this was a single gunshot wound.

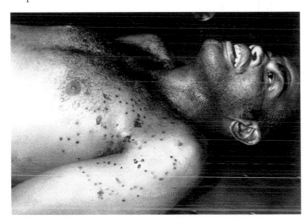

FIGURE 7.18 This man was shot multiple times from the same gun. The wounds to the shoulder and chest were caused by "rat" shot or "snake" shot. See next photo.

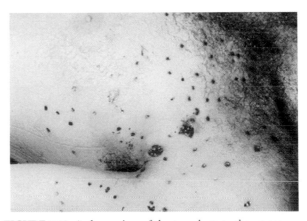

FIGURE 7.19 A closer view of the two shots to the upper chest. See next photo.

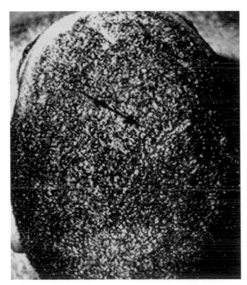

FIGURE 7.20 The graze (gutter) wound to the top of the head was caused by a single projectile. See next photo.

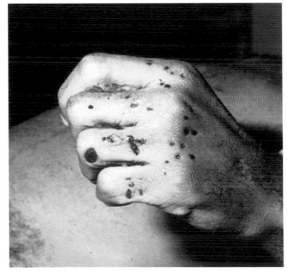

FIGURE 7.21 Wounds on the left hand were also caused by snake shot.

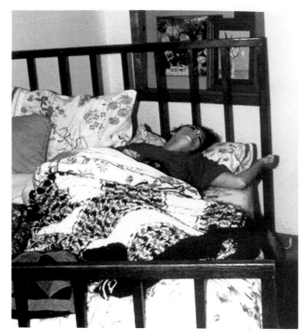

FIGURE 7.22 Law enforcement responded to a call and discovered a woman dead in bed from gunshot wounds to the abdomen. See next photo.

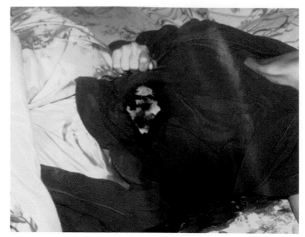

FIGURE 7.23 There were multiple shots to the abdomen with abundant gunpowder. A gun was next to her in the bed. See next photo.

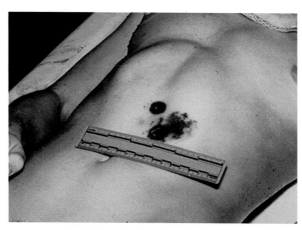

FIGURE 7.25 There were three loose contact wounds to the abdomen. One of the bullets hit the spleen. There were no other major organs damaged. See next photo.

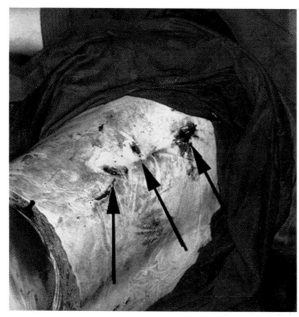

FIGURE 7.24 The arrows are pointing to the three exit wounds. All the bullets were found in the bed. See next photo.

FIGURE 7.26 On the kitchen table were papers indicating the woman was putting her affairs in order. The investigator now knew the manner could be ruled suicide.

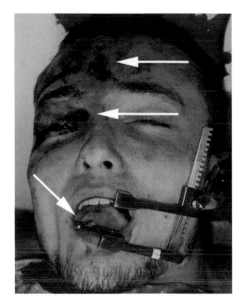

FIGURE 7.27 A suicide with two loose contact wounds to the head. The wounds are near the eye and on the forehead. The man left a suicide note at the scene. The lowest arrow points to a tongue piercing which can be seen on X-rays. See next photo.

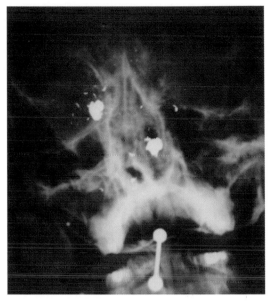

FIGURE 7.28 The X-ray shows the two bullets in the head and a piercing of the tongue by a "barbell" piece of jewelry. The bullet which entered near the eye travelled along the base of the brain, causing little damage. The shot to the forehead perforated the brain. See next photo.

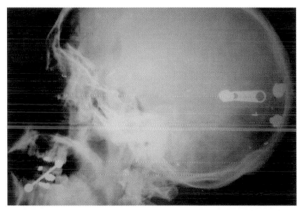

FIGURE 7.29 A side view of the bullets. The head of the zipper is from the bag he was in when the radiographs were taken.

FIGURE 7.30 In the dining room at the end of the foyer in this house were two bodies. The arrow points to a gun. See next photo.

FIGURE 7.31 The man was lying next to the woman, a pool of blood around his head. See next photo.

Chapter 8

SHOTGUN INJURIES

Unlike handguns and rifles which have lands-and-grooves cut on the inside of their barrels, shotguns have a smooth bore. Lands-and-grooves cause specific identifying features (rifling) on projectiles as they pass along the barrel. These markings allow examiners to test-fire weapons and compare test-fired bullets to those discovered in bodies. Since shotguns have no lands-and-grooves, their projectiles cannot be positively matched to those found at the scene or inside a body.

A shotgun cartridge contains pellets, gunpowder, and a wad that separates the pellets from the gunpowder. Some ammunition have plastic shot containers that hold the pellets and also act as the wad. The recovery of the wad or plastic shot container is important because they may be specific for certain types of ammunition. Shotguns usually fire pellets; however, slugs can also be used as ammunition.

The range (distance) of fire can usually be more easily determined in shotguns than in handguns or rifles. In addition to the presence or absence of gunpowder, the presence or absence of pellet spread aids in the distance determination. However, it is still important to test-fire the same gun and ammunition that was used in the shooting to determine an accurate comparison with the distance in question.

FIGURE 8.1 A shotgun blast can be very destructive. This man stuck the gun in his mouth.

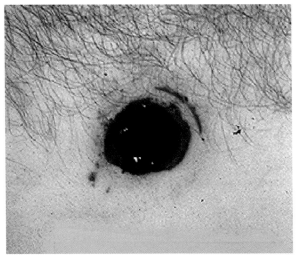

FIGURE 8.2 Tight contact shotgun wound of the chest. All of the gunpowder is inside the wound. The wound edges are abraded and there is a thin linear abrasion on the upper right from the muzzle.

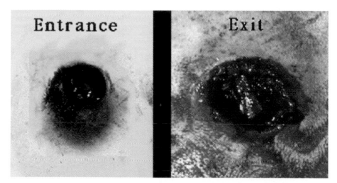

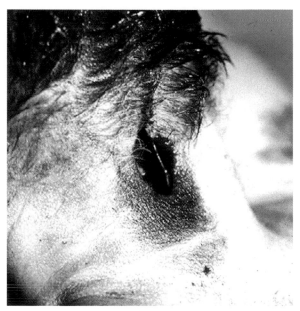

FIGURE 8.3 Loose contact shotgun wound and a larger, more ragged exit wound.

FIGURE 8.4 Loose contact shotgun wound to the back of the head and neck. The decedent was essentially executed during a robbery.

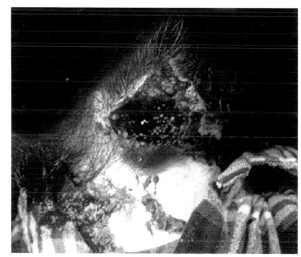

FIGURE 8.5 This loose contact suicide wound to the neck is larger than expected because the neck was bent over the barrel. Most of the decedent's face was blown out.

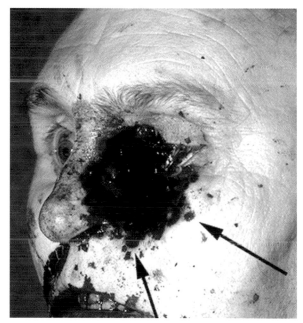

FIGURE 8.6 This "cookie cutter" type wound shows a few separate pellet injuries forming as the distance increases. This is not a suicide.

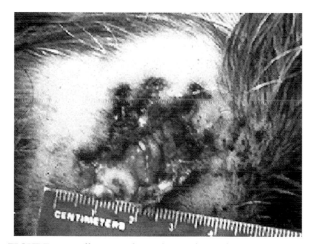

FIGURE 8.7 Pellet spread may be used to aid in distance determination when there is no more gunpowder. In this case, the pellets are beginning to spread. Once again, the distance may be determined with accuracy only if the same ammunition and weapon are test-fired.

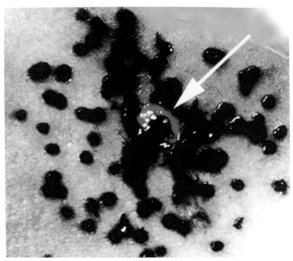

FIGURE 8.8 The central defect may be small as the weapon is moved further away from the body when fired. The wad was discovered in the body.

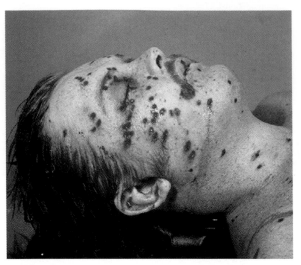

FIGURE 8.9 The spread of pellets indicates a considerable distance; however, the distance is affected by the choke of the weapon. Adjacent to the corner of the mouth is an abrasion from the wad.

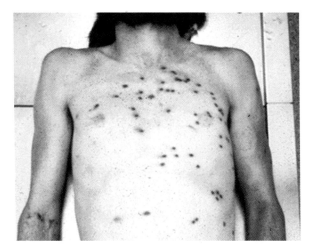

FIGURE 8.10 This man was shot by a policeman from across the yard. Only three pellets traveled deep into the body. Unfortunately, these pellets entered the heart.

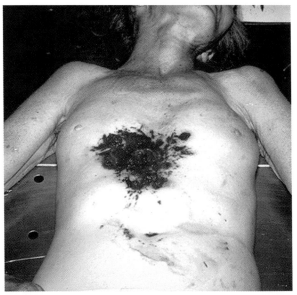

FIGURE 8.11 This woman was shot with a shotgun. The wound does not appear like a typical shotgun wound. Many of the ragged defects were not caused by pellets. See next photo.

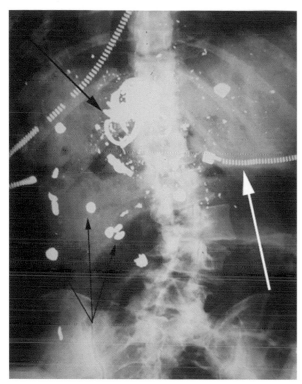

FIGURE 8.12 An X-ray revealed multiple pellets and other odd-shaped metallic objects. These other objects were keys and the ring they were on. The woman was wearing a ring of keys around her neck. The white arrow points to a zipper. She was X-rayed in a body bag.

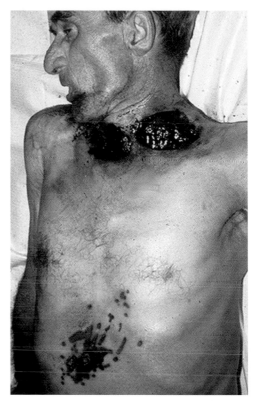

FIGURE 8.13 This man had two shotgun wounds. The lower one in the abdomen reveals a pellet direction up to the decedent's left. The neck blast was from a closer distance. The wound on the left side of the neck is the exit wound.

FIGURE 8.14 The gray marks on this bone are lead markings from shotgun pellet impacts. No pellets were remaining in the body; however, this finding proved the person was killed with a shotgun.

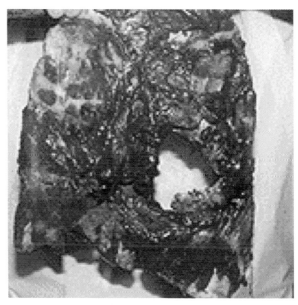

FIGURE 8.15 A relatively small external wound can be accompanied by a larger defect in the body. The external entrance wound in this case was half the size of the defect in the chest plate, as seen here.

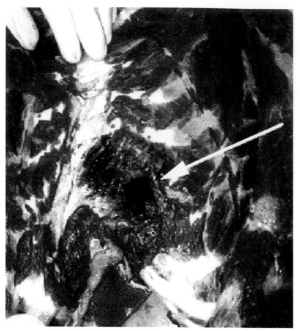

FIGURE 8.16 This is another defect in a chest wall. This one is approximately the same size as the external wound.

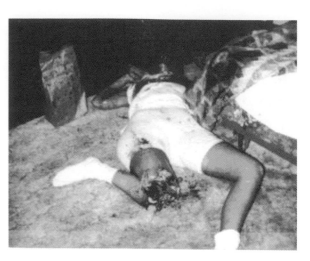

FIGURE 8.17 This is the scene of a woman shot twice by her estranged husband She was killed with shotgun slugs and not pellets. See next photo.

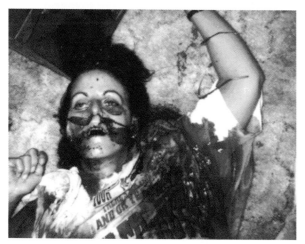

FIGURE 8.18 Scene close-up revealing powder on the shirt and abundant blood. See next photo.

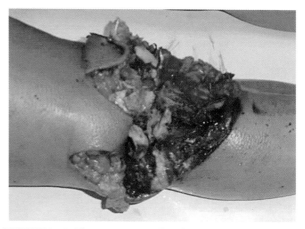

FIGURE 8.19 The woman was shot first in the right knee. There is a slight amount of gunpowder on the inferior aspect of the wound. See next photo.

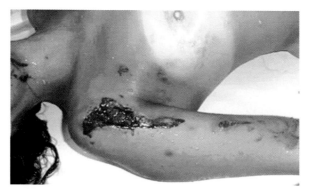

FIGURE 8.20 Fragments of bone caused damage to the right upper arm. See next photo.

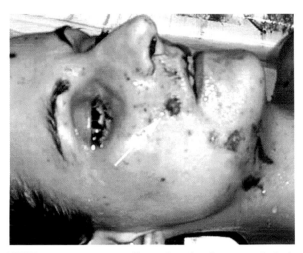

FIGURE 8.21 Fragments of bone from her knee were imbedded in her face (arrow). This gives an indication of her defensive posturing at the time of the shot. See next photo.

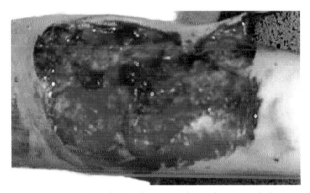

FIGURE 8.22 This is her right arm where the second shot began. This wound is superficial. There is gunpowder on the inferior aspect (to the right). See next photo.

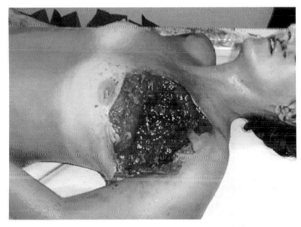

FIGURE 8.23 The main charge from the second shot entered the left side of the chest, creating this huge defect. There were a few small exit wounds on the left back. Metal fragments from the slug were located in the muscle and tissue of the back.

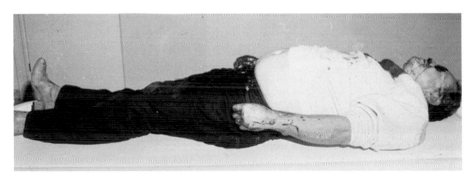

FIGURE 8.24 This man and his best friend were arguing over his daughter. The assailant said he shot at this man from about 10' away as the decedent was rising out of his sofa and coming after him with a knife. See next photo.

Chapter 9

ASPHYXIA (SUFFOCATION) AND DROWNING

ASPHYXIA

Asphyxia means death due to lack of oxygen to the brain. The following are the different ways a person can asphyxiate:

1. Compression of the neck (hanging and strangulation)
2. Blockage of the airway (suffocation, gagging)
3. Compression of the chest, neck, or face (postural or positional asphyxia)
4. Chemical and lack of available oxygen in the atmosphere

Compression of the neck

In hanging (usually suicide), the neck can be compressed by rope, wire, or articles of clothing. Pressure on the neck will usually occlude the vasculature, but not necessarily the airway (larynx or trachea). Very little pressure is needed to occlude the blood vessels. It is a misconception that the airway must be occluded to asphyxiate. Ruptured blood vessels in the tissues after prolonged hanging, especially in the lower extremities, are called Tardieu spots.

The neck can also be compressed manually by strangulation or throttling. An assailant must compress either the airway or the blood vessels to render a victim unconscious. The time it takes to render an individual unconscious is quite variable (seconds to over a minute). Once a victim becomes unconscious, pressure must be continued in order to cause death.

Signs of trauma to the neck are generally evident in manual strangulation and hanging. There may be contusions or abrasions but rarely lacerations. An object used to compress the neck often leaves an abraded, imprinted mark. If the ligature is thin like a rope, the depressed mark on the neck is usually apparent and the pattern can be matched to the particular ligature. If the ligature is wide, like a towel or shirt, there will be no specific pattern of the ligature. There may be superficial fingernail cuts from either the victim or assailant; however, they are usually from the victim.

Pinpoint hemorrhages, or petechiae, are commonly present in the eyes after manual compression of the neck. Petechiae may be on either the bulb of the eye, or on the lids, or both. Petechiae may also be found on the face, especially the forehead, and around the eyes. They are caused by the buildup of vascular pressure which causes capillaries to rupture. They are not often found in suicidal hanging. Petechiae are not specific for asphyxiation and may occur in sudden natural death.

Autoerotic deaths

A unique subgroup of asphyxial deaths are autoerotic deaths which occur during purposeful attempts to reduce blood flow to the brain by neck compression during masturbation. Any object which compresses the neck can be used. Most of the time a towel or some soft object is placed between the ligature and the neck to prevent visible scrapes or bruises. The diagnosis is readily made at the scene because the decedent is usually naked with pornographic material nearby. Often there is evidence of repeated behavior at the scene, such as worn grooves in the rafters where ropes or pulleys have been placed. The manner of death is accidental.

Blockage of the airway (suffocation, aspiration, gagging)

If the airway is blocked, then oxygen cannot get into the lungs, and asphyxiation results. A pillow or hand, for instance, can be placed over the mouth, prevent a person from breathing, and cause suffocation. An unchewed peanut or small parts of toys can become lodged in an infant's or child's airway. Individuals without teeth or with a history of stroke or other debilitating disease may have trouble chewing and aspirate food into the airway. Those under the influence of alcohol are also more likely to aspirate. There are usually no signs of trauma in these deaths.

Compression of the chest, neck, or face (postural or positional asphyxia)

Postural asphyxiation occurs when a person cannot breathe because of an inability to move one's chest, or the airway is compressed against the neck or face. This type of circumstance is commonly seen during motor vehicle accidents when the vehicle overturns on a victim or a driver may become trapped between the steering wheel and seat. There may be surprisingly few injuries except for other signs of blunt trauma and petechiae of the eyes and face.

Chemical and lack of available oxygen in the atmosphere

If the atmosphere's oxygen is replaced by another chemical or gas, or if a person's red blood cells are unable to deliver oxygen to bodily tissues, a person will asphyxiate. Depletion of atmospheric oxygen usually occurs in a relatively closed environment. Examples include gas which can accumulate and displace oxygen in improperly vented mine shafts, sewers, or chemical storage tanks. It is common to encounter multiple deaths in such cases because rescuers can also be overcome by fumes and lack of oxygen.

Examples of chemical asphyxia by interfering with oxygen delivery to the tissues include carbon monoxide and cyanide. When a car is left running in a closed garage, carbon monoxide from burning gasoline competes with oxygen on the red blood cells. Carbon monoxide can incapacitate a person very quickly. The most common cause of death in fires is carbon monoxide poisoning. Cyanide causes livor mortis to be red as in carbon monoxide poisoning. The cyanide gas may smell like bitter almonds. Both deaths can occur quickly, especially cyanide poisoning.

DROWNING

The diagnosis of drowning tends to be one of exclusion. Other than some work with diatoms, there are no good drowning tests to prove a person drowned; the autopsy is usually negative. To make the diagnosis, the body is usually wet, or is found in water. There may be injuries from being in the water, such as tears and scrapes of the skin from impacts against boats or bridges. Occasionally, marine life, more often in salt water, may feed on the skin of the face, especially around the mouth, nose, and ears. Abrasions may be found on the forehead, knees, and backs of hands from a body scraping against the bottom of the lake or pool. There may be no external signs of trauma. Froth in the nose and mouth may be present. Wrinkling of the skin on the hands and feet is typical. Injuries to the body may occur from CPR attempts or from removing the body from the water. Internally, there may be heavy, wet lungs in those individuals who drown in salt water, but this is not always the case in fresh water drownings.

FIGURE 9.1 There may be blood on the clothing and relaxation of the bladder and bowels in people who hang themselves. It is also common for the decedent's feet to be touching the floor or ground.

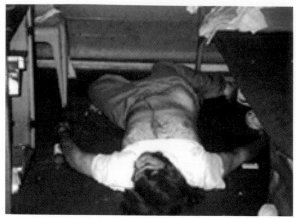

FIGURE 9.2 Most scene photographs show the people after they have already been taken down from the hanging position. See next photo.

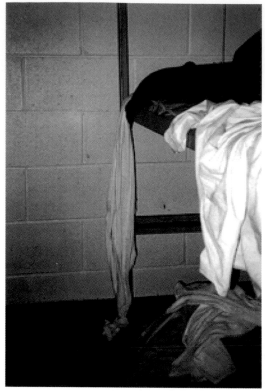

FIGURE 9.3 The man in the previous photo was not discovered hanging. His buttocks were on the floor when he was found.

FIGURE 9.4 This man hanged himself. His left foot is on the floor and his right is resting on the chair. See next photo.

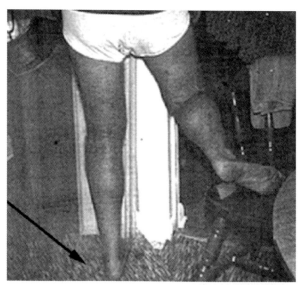

FIGURE 9.5 The feet on the floor or other objects are not an unusual finding. See next photo.

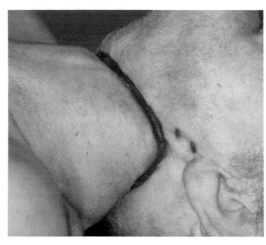

FIGURE 9.6 The ligature mark is distinct and forms an upside-down "V." The ligature mark may have a pattern of the object (in this case a rope) or it may be very indistinct. See next photo.

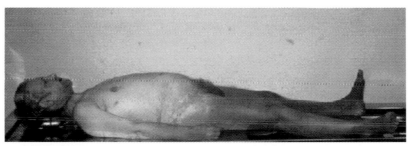

FIGURE 9.7 The livor mortis is as expected. It is concentrated in the dependent extremities. See next photo.

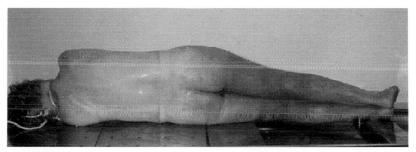

FIGURE 9.8 A posterior view also shows the dependent lividity. See next photo.

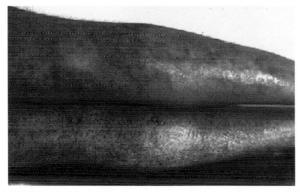

FIGURE 9.9 The left leg has many ruptured capillaries called "Tardieu spots." Notice the right leg does not have the spots because it was resting on the chair. These spots are also seen in other parts of the body when the decedent has been dead for an extended period of time. See next photo.

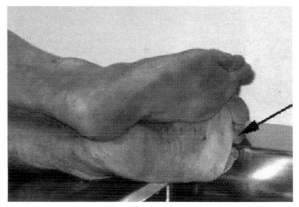

FIGURE 9.10 The bottom of the feet also reveal which foot was resting on the chair and which was in contact with the floor. The ball of the left foot (arrow) is pale because it was resting firmly against the floor.

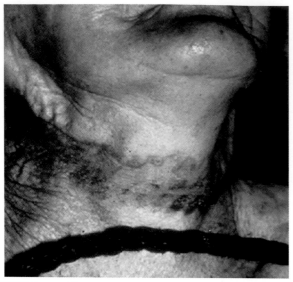

FIGURE 9.11 The rope pattern on this neck is very distinct and matches the rope. The pattern on the neck is wider than the rope because the folds of skin partially surrounded the ligature.

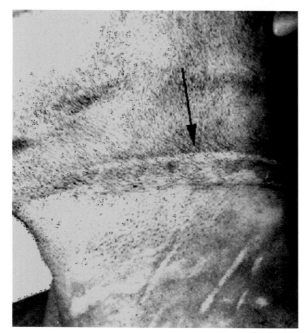

FIGURE 9.13 A shoestring wrapped twice around the neck caused these pale marks with adjacent hemorrhage.

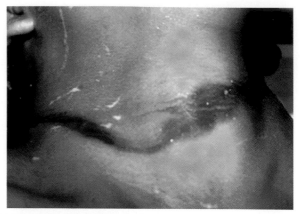

FIGURE 9.12 This is a typical nonpatterned abraded ligature mark which is commonly caused by objects such as towels, shirts, sheets, trousers, etc.

FIGURE 9.14 Sometimes determining manner of death is difficult. This is probably an accident; however, this cannot be stated with certainty. The boy may have been experimenting to see how it feels to choke.

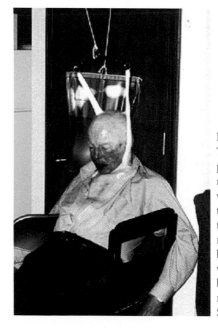

FIGURE 9.15 This retired physician had neck problems for which he used traction to ease the pain. Autopsy revealed he had a bad heart. There was no reason to believe he committed suicide. See next photo.

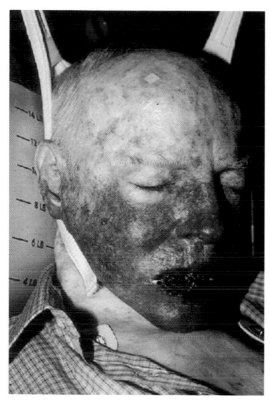

FIGURE 9.16 Lividity is on his lower face as expected. His lips and tongue have dried. There were no soft tissue hemorrhages in the neck and there were no petechiae of the eyes.

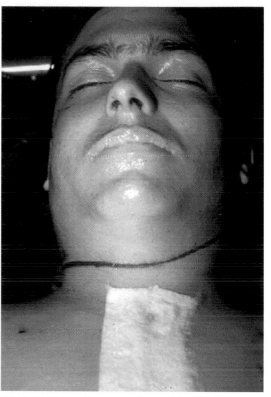

FIGURE 9.17 This military man hanged himself with a shoestring. He was autopsied in Europe (notice the lack of a Y-shaped incision). Interestingly, his neck organs had not been removed or examined.

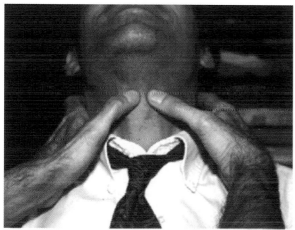

FIGURE 9.18 The hand position of the assailant on this model suggests one method of how people are strangled. Most people die from the pressure on the blood vessels and not from collapsing the larynx and trachea. See next photo.

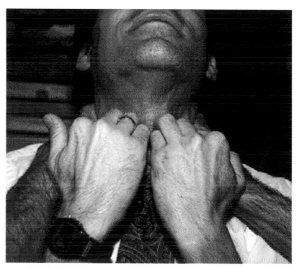

FIGURE 9.19 The victim may grasp the assailant's hands, leaving fingernail marks on his neck.

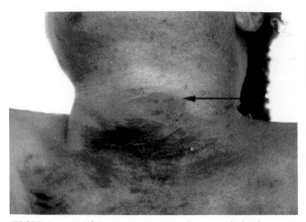

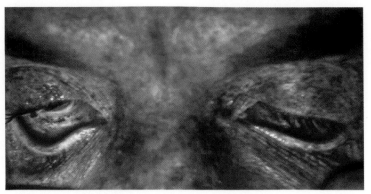

FIGURE 9.20 This man was manually strangled. There are contusions on the lower part of the neck and fingernail marks (arrow) above the contusions. There were numerous soft tissue hemorrhages and petechiae of the eyes.

FIGURE 9.21 The pinpoint hemorrhages in the this man's eyes and on the outside of his eyelids are called petechiae. Petechiae are not specific for strangulation. They can be found in other forms of asphyxiation and sudden death.

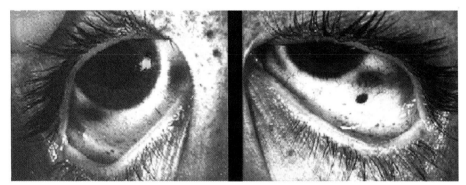

FIGURE 9.22 The petechiae in this boy's eyes occurred when he accidentally hanged himself.

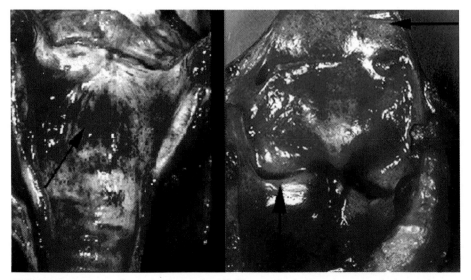

FIGURE 9.23 Hemorrhages in the trachea (left) may also be seen in strangulation and other asphyxial deaths. The lower arrow in the right photo points to the vocal cords while the upper arrow points to petechiae in the epiglottis.

FIGURE 9.24 The small hyoid bone is located high in the neck under the chin. The pathologist looks for injury to this structure because it is commonly fractured in a manual strangulation.

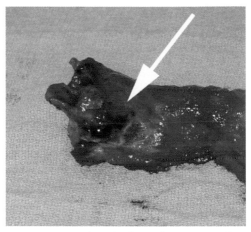

FIGURE 9.25 Hemorrhage in the neck organs may be present (arrow). See next photo.

FIGURE 9.26 There is hemorrhage in the base of this tongue (arrow) caused by manual strangulation.

FIGURE 9.27 This man was killed by his daughter's boyfriend. The assailant said he strangled the man with a come-a-long during the fight. See next photo.

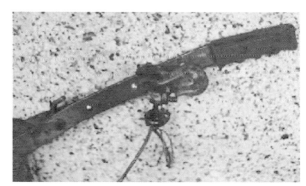

FIGURE 9.28 This is a come-a-long. It is used to move a heavy object toward another object. One end is attached to a support and the hook is attached to the object to be moved. See next photo.

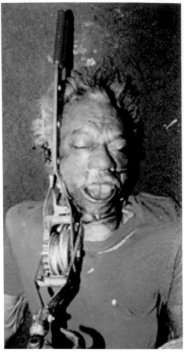

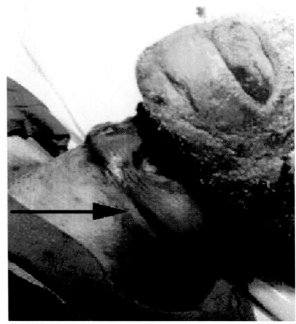

FIGURE 9.29 The come-a-long is an unwieldy piece of equipment. It cannot be hooked and cranked quickly during a fight. The assailant lied about this. See next photo.

FIGURE 9.30 A closer look at the neck reveals a second abraded ligature mark (arrow) below the area where the come-a-long was tightened. This proves the man's neck was compressed prior to the assailant's use of the come-a-long.

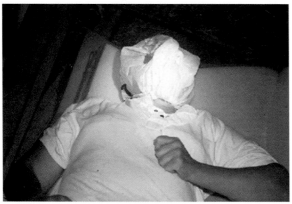

FIGURE 9.31 Asphyxiation by occluding the airway with a bag. This method of suicide is seen more commonly in the elderly.

FIGURE 9.32 The car this man was working on fell off the concrete blocks, compressing his neck. See next photo.

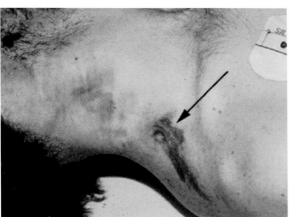

FIGURE 9.33 There were few serious injuries. The arrow points to the worst of his external injuries. See next photo.

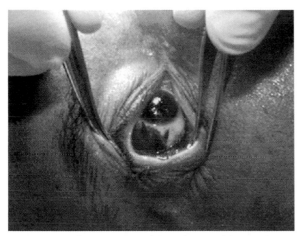

FIGURE 9.34 The pressure on his neck caused impressive hemorrhages in his eyes. The hemorrhages were not the typical petechiae seen in manual strangulation.

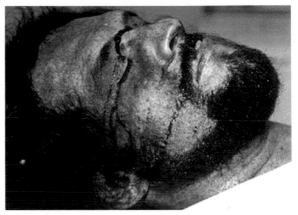

FIGURE 9.35 This man was caught under his truck after a traffic accident. His face is dark purple from blood forced up to his head under pressure. He died because he could not breathe due to compression of his chest.

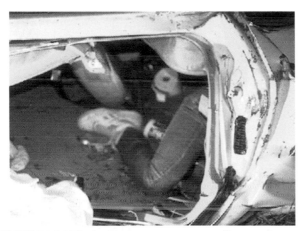

FIGURE 9.36 The body of a young man was discovered upside down in his car after the car rolled over. See next photo.

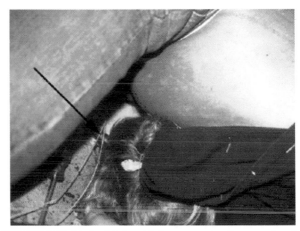

FIGURE 9.37 Notice his head is bent completely around and resting on his chest. The autopsy revealed no injuries. His neck was not broken and there were no petechiae. This is another example of postural asphyxiation.

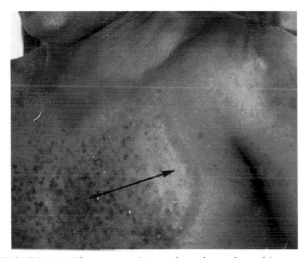

FIGURE 9.38 The arrow points to the only mark on this man's body after he was discovered compressed between the cab of his truck and the ground after an accident. He had petechiae, but there were no internal injuries.

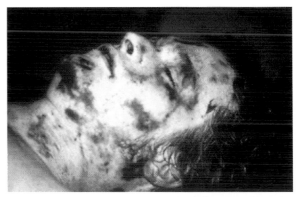

FIGURE 9.39 The abrasions on this boy's face were his only injuries. He died of suffocation after his face was compressed against another person's back.

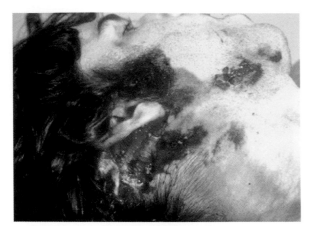

FIGURE 9.40 These injuries to the neck appear significant; however, there was little internal damage. His head was caught between the floor of an elevator and the outside door of the elevator shaft. His head was bent enough to prevent breathing.

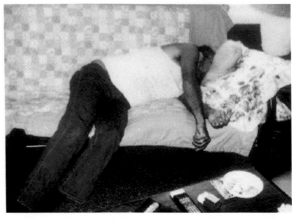

FIGURE 9.41 This alcoholic fell asleep with his head on the pillow. See next photo.

FIGURE 9.42 His nose and mouth were occluded by the pillow, and he suffocated. The autopsy was unremarkable except for signs of alcoholism. The scene investigation was essential in determining the proper manner of death (accident).

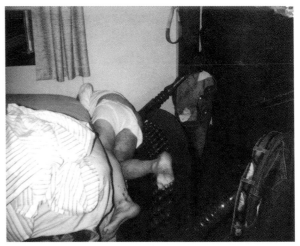

FIGURE 9.43 Another case of positional asphyxiation. This alcoholic fell out of bed and ended up in a position in which he could not breathe. See next photo.

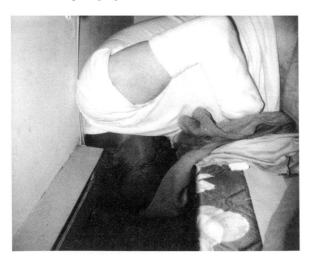

FIGURE 9.44 His head was bent enough to prevent adequate aeration. Notice the dark discoloration of his head.

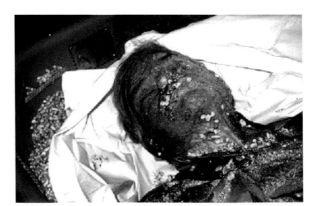

FIGURE 9.45 Death due to occlusion of the airway. This man fell into a silo while shoveling corn.

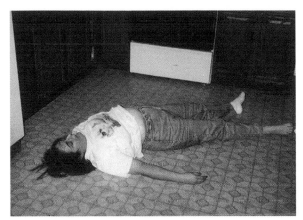

FIGURE 9.46 This woman was discovered dead at home by her mother. She was a chronic alcoholic who was known to swallow large quantities of food and then drink alcohol. She did this because she felt the food would decrease the absorption of the alcohol, thereby allowing her to remain drunk for longer periods of time. See next photo.

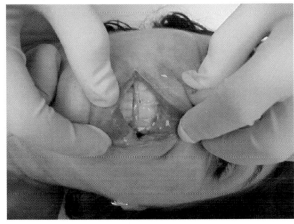

FIGURE 9.47 A few fragments of food were in her mouth and on her face. See next photo.

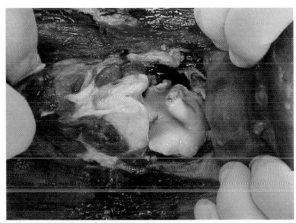

FIGURE 9.48 A bolus of turkey was lodged in her airway. See next photo.

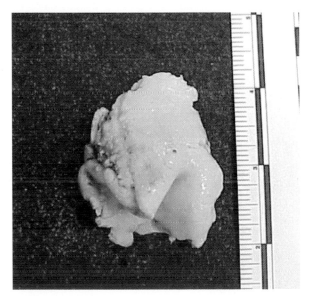

FIGURE 9.49 The wad of meat measured over 2" × 1.5" in total dimension.

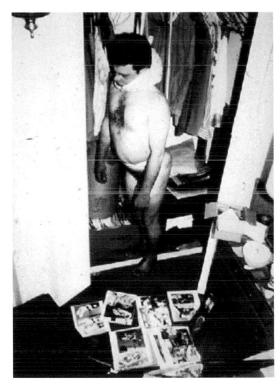

FIGURE 9.50 Autoerotic asphyxiation. This young man died from compression of the neck after he lost consciousness during masturbation. There were pornographic magazines on the floor and a full-length mirror leaning against the bed. See next photo.

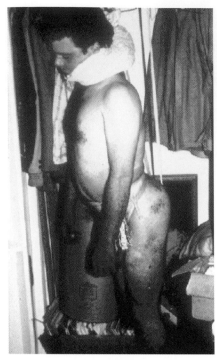

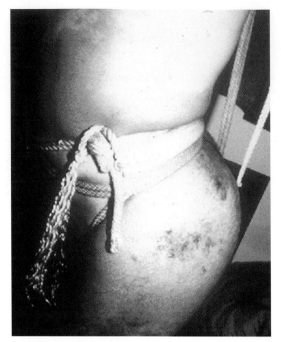

FIGURE 9.52 He had devised a slipknot to help him if he needed a quick escape. See next photo.

FIGURE 9.51 There was a towel around the neck to prevent abrasions and the ropes were tied in an elaborate swing-like configuration. See next photo.

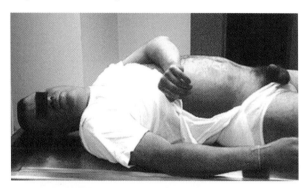

FIGURE 9.53 This soldier also died during masturbation. He had a bag over his head during the act and died from a lack of oxygen.

FIGURE 9.54 Carbon monoxide poisoning. The man who died in this car ran a hose from the exhaust into the interior.

FIGURE 9.55 Most carbon monoxide asphyxiations occur in a garage. This one occurred in the open and no hoses were involved. See next photo.

FIGURE 9.56 The back seat of the car was removed; a hole was cut in the floor. See next photo.

FIGURE 9.57 The tailpipe was bent up to fit into the hole.

FIGURE 9.58 This is a case in which a hose was brought into the truck through the back window and secured in place with tape.

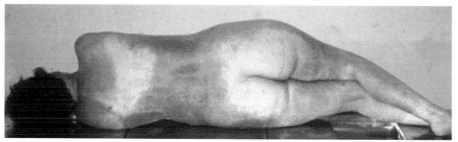

FIGURE 9.59 Carbon monoxide poisoning causes red livor mortis. Red livor mortis also occurs in cyanide poisoning and from the cold.

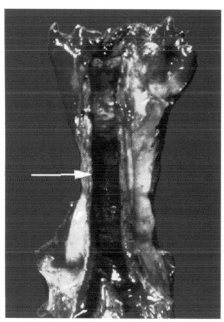

FIGURE 9.60 Soot or smoke in the trachea is a sign of inhalation at the time of the fire. The person was alive during the fire.

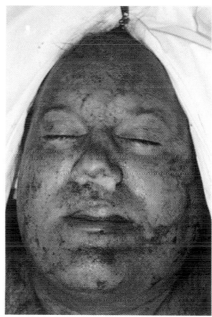

FIGURE 9.61 Drowning. Foam in the nose is a classic sign of drowning. It may be the only sign of drowning on the body. Some drowning victims have abrasions of the face, forehead, hands, feet, and knees.

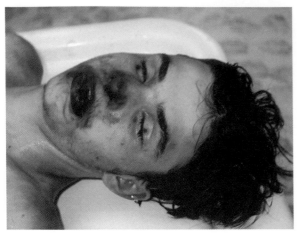

FIGURE 9.62 There are numerous abrasions, contusions, and lacerations to this boy's face and mouth. He and his uncle drowned in a shallow river during an afternoon outing with family. See next photo.

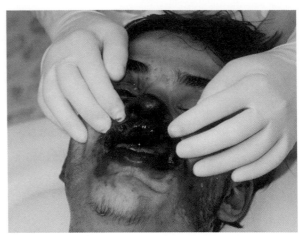

FIGURE 9.63 The boy's uncle also had similar injuries to his face and mouth. See next photo.

FIGURE 9.64 This is an underwater photograph showing none of the injuries to the young man's face that were evident at the autopsy. These injuries did not occur during a fight or the struggle for survival.

FIGURE 9.65 This man drowned and the body was not discovered for three weeks in the wintertime. The injuries to the body came after death.

FIGURE 9.66 Abundant moss covered most of this young man's body after only three weeks in a pond. See next photo.

FIGURE 9.67 The moss was especially thick on the trunk. It had to be scraped away to look for injuries. See next photo.

FIGURE 9.68 There was also plenty of moss on the face. See next photo.

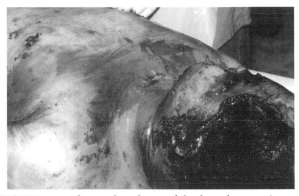

FIGURE 9.69 The trunk and part of the face after scraping. See next photo.

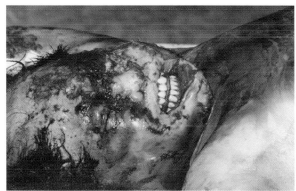

FIGURE 9.70 Another angle of the face after scraping, with good exposure of the mouth and teeth.

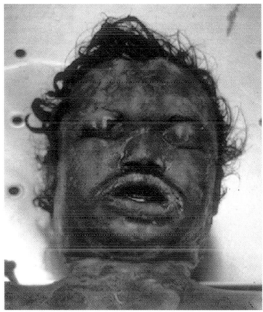

FIGURE 9.71 This young white man drowned in a river and was not found for 4–5 days after death in the early fall. There were no signs of drowning.

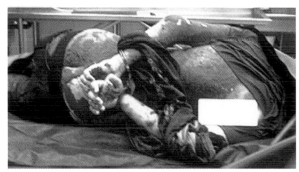

FIGURE 9.72 This man drowned after he was handcuffed, struck in the head, and forced into a river.

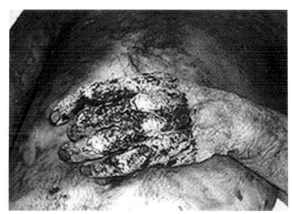

FIGURE 9.73 Wrinkling of the skin from drowning. Notice the rest of the body does not have this change. The feet had skin slippage like the hands.

FIGURE 9.74 This woman was discovered in a tub full of water after the police went to her home to notify her of her boyfriend's death. He committed suicide by inhaling auto exhaust. See next photo.

FIGURE 9.75 A radio was in the water, suggesting electrocution. See next photo.

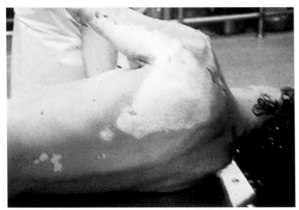

FIGURE 9.76 The water had caused significant skin slippage. See next photo.

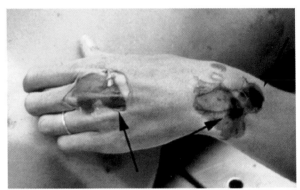

FIGURE 9.77 There were abrasions of the left hand and wrist. See next photo.

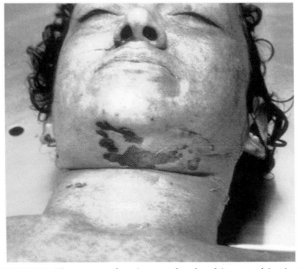

FIGURE 9.78 There were abrasions under the chin, petechiae in the eyes, and soft tissue hemorrhage of the neck. She had been strangled and placed in the bathtub with a radio to make it appear as if she died of electrocution. The boyfriend strangled her and then committed suicide.

Chapter 10

THERMAL INJURIES

Thermal injuries are described according to depth and degree of total body surface damaged. The degree of injury is either first- (sunburn), second- (sunburn with blisters), third- (soft tissue injury which heals by scarring), or fourth-degree (charring of the tissues). The total body surface injury is quantitated by physicians according to the rule of nines, which gives a total number of area burned. Younger individuals can withstand more injury than older ones; still, this also depends on the part of the body burned. Burns affecting the airways cause more complications than those areas burned on other parts of the body.

Most fire deaths are due to carbon monoxide (CO) poisoning, not direct thermal injury. Exposure to CO can be fatal within minutes. Thermal effects to the body may be slight or severe. The degree of heat does not dictate how long a person survives during a fire. The extent of damage depends on the length of time a decedent is exposed to flames and how close a body is to a fire.

The most important factor in any fire death investigation is determining whether an individual was dead before a fire started (suspected homicide). This is determined by examining the airway for the inhalation of smoke and the measurement of CO content in the blood. These evaluations can only be determined during and after autopsy.

CO will cause cherry red livor mortis. Occasionally, the CO will be negative as is in an explosion which causes death rapidly. A negative CO might initially be confusing, but a quality scene investigation should resolve any problems.

Individuals may die later in the hospital from complications such as inhalation injuries to the airways, infections, and fluid and electrolyte disorders. Skin burns may range from partial or full thickness to charring and incineration.

Heat artifacts include:

1. Changes in height and weight of the body.
2. Hair color changes — Brown hair may become red and blonde may become gray; black hair does not change color.
3. Thermal fractures — These are difficult to differentiate from antemortem fractures.
4. Skin splits with evisceration of organs.

Most fire deaths should be X-rayed so that foreign objects will not be overlooked. Blood can usually be obtained from a body no matter how badly it is burned.

FIGURE 10.1 Most thermal injuries occur from structure fires. The most important question to answer is if the decedent was alive or dead during the fire. The answer to this question enables the investigator to distinguish between homicide and other manners of death.

FIGURE 10.2 Thermal injuries may be encountered in traffic accidents. The main questions are to decide if the person was alive, dying, or dead at the time of the fire and accident.

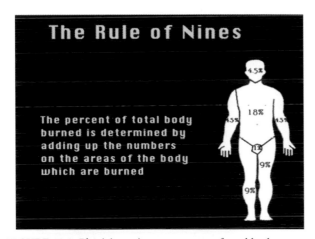

FIGURE 10.3 Physicians give percentages of total body surface burned based on the rule of nines.

FIGURE 10.4 A first-degree burn is similar to a sunburn without blistering. A second-degree burn has blistering. Neither type will heal with a scar.

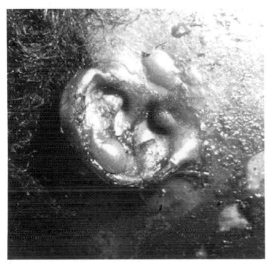

FIGURE 10.5 Blistering with thickening (induration) of the skin and tissues is a third-degree burn. This will usually heal with a scar.

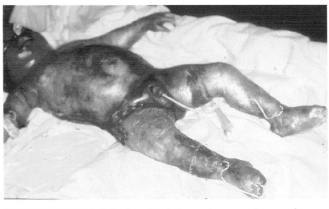

FIGURE 10.6 This baby has third-degree burns and some charring (fourth-degree) burns. As a rule, younger individuals can survive more serious burns than older people. Relatively minor thermal injuries can cause death in the elderly.

FIGURE 10.7 This is fourth-degree thermal injury. There is diffuse charring of the body. An autopsy should be performed in these cases if warranted.

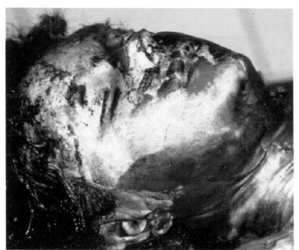

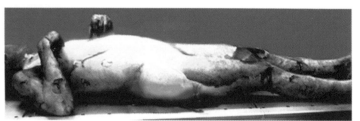

FIGURE 10.9 Carbon monoxide (CO) poisoning will cause the skin to turn red. Direct thermal injury may also cause the skin to be red. The larynx and/or CO concentrations still need to be checked to determine the cause of death.

FIGURE 10.8 Most people die in fires by carbon monoxide poisoning from inhaling smoke. Smoke in the nostrils and mouth does not prove the person died from inhalation. The larynx must be examined to check for the presence of smoke.

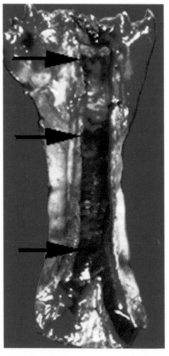

FIGURE 10.10 The abundant amount of smoke on this man's face suggests he died from inhaling smoke. His face is covered with smoke because of the smoke in the fire. This does not prove he died from smoke inhalation. See next photo.

FIGURE 10.11 This is the larynx (upper arrow) and the trachea (windpipe). The lower arrows point to carbon material in the trachea from inhaling smoke. The presence of smoke in the lower larynx and trachea proves the decedent was alive during the fire.

FIGURE 10.13 The heat will cause bones to break and skin to split. The presence of postmortem thermal fractures (arrow) should not be confused with antemortem injuries. See next photo.

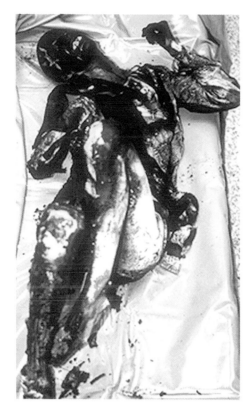

FIGURE 10.12 Fire will cause the joints to contract. The arms and legs may be bent. This "pugilist" (boxer) appearance makes the decedent appear as if she were fighting at the time of her death. These contractures are all postmortem.

FIGURE 10.14 Thermal fractures may be very difficult to distinguish from antemortem fractures. The pathologist should be conservative when making this distinction.

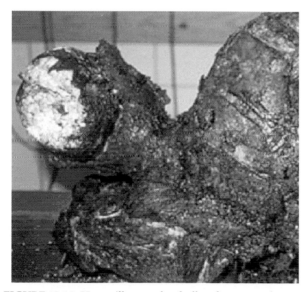

FIGURE 10.15 Heat will cause the skull to fracture and come apart. The underlying brain may be fragmented and cooked. This should not be confused with antemortem trauma to the head.

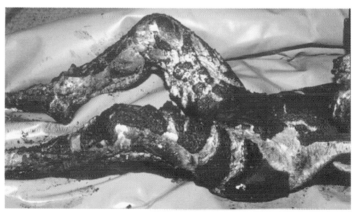

FIGURE 10.16 Skin splitting is a common artifact of thermal injury. The splits may be confused with sharp force injury.

FIGURE 10.17 This body has charring, skin splits, and the pugilistic attitude in the upper extremities.

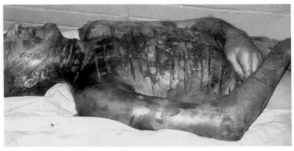

FIGURE 10.18 The multiple cuts across this man's chest and abdomen were caused by the surgeon and not fire. This procedure helps to ease the pressure buildup in the tissues which can cause muscle and nerve damage.

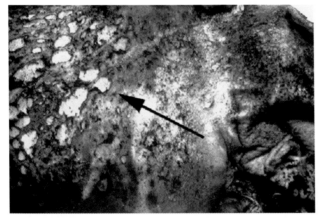

FIGURE 10.19 The heat may cause the skin to bubble and blister. These are postmortem injuries.

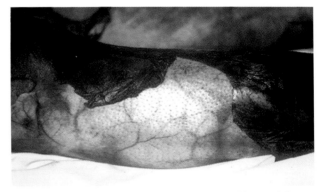

FIGURE 10.20 The heat may cause the external layer of the skin to slip and peel off the body.

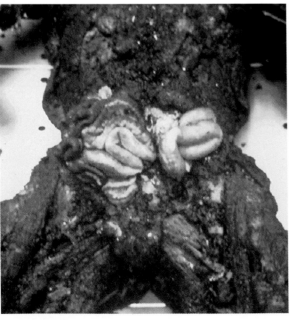

FIGURE 10.21 The splitting of the skin and tissue may cause organs to become exposed. This evisceration of organs should not be mistaken for antemortem injuries.

FIGURE 10.22 This child was one of two children found dead in a bedroom. The body had thermal injuries to 100% of the total body surface. See next photo.

FIGURE 10.23 There was a marked amount of hemorrhage just under the skull. This epidural hemorrhage would be suspicious of blunt trauma injury if the child had not died in a fire. This particular type of hemorrhage is an artifact of the fire. See next photo.

FIGURE 10.24 A closer look shows the hemorrhage distributed over the entire surface of the dura mater. An antemortem epidural hemorrhage is thicker and more of a discrete entity. Subsequent examination of the brain in this case revealed no injury to the brain.

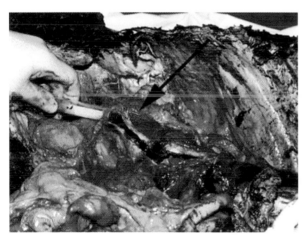

FIGURE 10.25 No matter how badly damaged a body, a blood specimen can usually be obtained. The redness of the tissues in this case suggests the person died of carbon monoxide poisoning. The blood test will confirm this opinion.

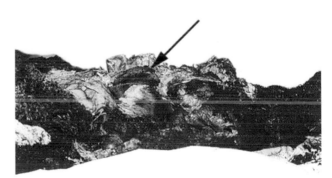

FIGURE 10.26 Organs are still present and can be examined in these badly damaged remains.

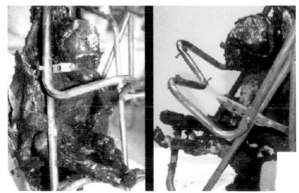

FIGURE 10.27 Scene photos may be important. This child was still strapped in her car seat when the fire killed her.

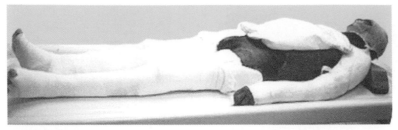

FIGURE 10.28 This man appeared badly burned, but he died from a reaction to an antibiotic. This reaction, called "toxic epidermal necrolysis," could be mistaken for a thermal injury if the history is not known. See next photo.

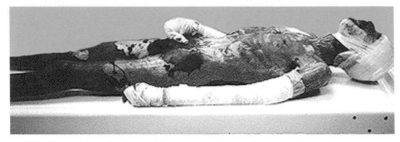

FIGURE 10.29 Much of the skin has peeled away from the body due to the drug reaction. See next photo.

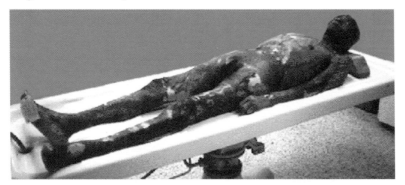

FIGURE 10.30 Another view of this catastrophic reaction to a drug.

FIGURE 10.31 All of these people died suddenly when a fire was started downstairs. Notice there is no fire damage to this room or the bodies. Victims may succumb to other noxious gases besides carbon monoxide.

FIGURE 10.32 Two bodies were buried in this casket. A father and his son were in a tractor trailer when it was struck by another truck. Eighteen months after burial, they had to be disinterred because of a civil suit. The question was whether they were alive or dead at the time of the accident. See next photo.

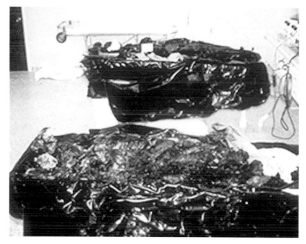

FIGURE 10.33 Both bodies had been badly burned and were decomposed. See next photo.

FIGURE 10.35 This is the block of neck, lungs, and heart. See next photo.

FIGURE 10.34 This body still had a head and neck while the other's head and neck had been burned away. See next photo.

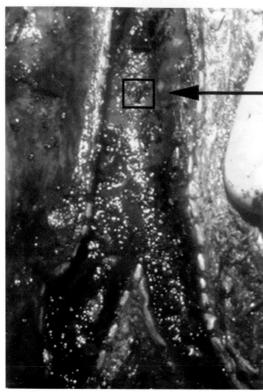

FIGURE 10.37 There was no neck to evaluate in the other body. However, the liver was bright red. It is usually brown. The examiner concluded the red discoloration was caused by carbon monoxide and ruled this person was also alive at the time of the accident.

FIGURE 10.36 Fortunately, black pigment could still be found in the trachea (arrow). This proved this man was alive at the time of the fire. See next photo.

Chapter 11

ELECTROCUTION, DRUGS, AND THE ENVIRONMENT

ELECTROCUTION

Electrocution is not always an easy diagnosis to make. The history and circumstances of death are vitally important because low voltage deaths frequently cause no injuries on the body. On the other hand, high voltage deaths are easier to diagnose because of obvious burns.

The cause of death from electrocution is related to the amount of current (or amperage) flowing through a body. Although both direct and alternating currents can be lethal, most deaths occur from contact with alternating currents having low voltages such as 110 or 220 usually found in homes.

There needs to be a complete circuit from the power source to the ground for death to occur. A person will not become electrocuted if insulated from the ground. The direction the path takes in the body determines if the shock will be fatal. An arrhythmia is likely if current travels through the heart.

External injuries may vary tremendously. The extent of external wound damage is dependent upon the amount of current and its duration. If a current is spread over a wide area for a short duration there will not be any injuries to the skin. Clothing may be damaged so it must be retained for examination. The skin may be secondarily injured by burning clothes.

Low voltage tends to cause easily overlooked small burns especially on the hands and the feet. The lesions may be red, black, or white and inconspicuous, with depressed firm centers. High voltage deaths usually leave easily recognizable, deeply charred areas. Lesions may be present at the entrance and/or exit sites.

If someone dies while working with electrical equipment, the equipment needs to be tested by a qualified individual.

LIGHTNING

Lightning may kill by either a direct or an indirect strike. Injuries may be slight to nonexistent or quite impressive. The victim usually dies by heart stoppage. Metal on the clothing or body may heat up and cause secondary injuries. Occasionally, a red fern-like pattern may develop on the skin. This is only seen in electrocution and may disappear within hours of the death.

DRUGS

Drugs may be the cause of death, contribute to the cause of death, or contribute to the circumstances surrounding a death. There are many different types of drugs, both legal and illicit, that may be the cause of death. Any drug or chemical taken in excess can cause death. This includes illicit drugs, over-the-counter medicines, and prescription drugs.

Common drugs of abuse encountered in death cases include ethyl alcohol, barbiturates, pain killers, stimulants such as cocaine and methamphetamine, heroin, morphine, LSD, marijuana, and antidepressants. These drugs can readily be discovered through routine postmortem drug screens by testing blood, urine, or other tissues. Chemicals such as carbon monoxide and cyanide may be involved. Blood and urine are not usually tested for these chemicals; however, the circumstances of death may lead the examiner to suspect these chemicals as a cause of death (such as carbon monoxide in fire). Special samples such as hair may be needed to test for cases of heavy metal poisoning, such as arsenic.

Autopsy findings may vary from obvious signs of drug abuse to a negative autopsy. Chronic intravenous drug abusers have easily recognizable needle tracks while chronic alcoholics may have cirrhosis of the liver and bleeding abnormalities. Drugs as a cause of death should be suspected in a negative autopsy in which there is no obvious cause of death. As a general rule, all post-mortem examinations should include a drug screen because drugs may play a part in any type of death. Good investigation is needed to rule in or out the possibility of drugs playing a part in someone's death. Except for alcohol, any drug which contributes in any way to a person's death will change the manner of death from natural to accident, suicide, or homicide.

HYPERTHERMIA

Very few signs at autopsy will indicate a person died from hyperthermia. The most important sign is body temperature. If a body is found at a scene soon after death, an increased temperature will be evident. If a decedent is not found for many hours, or is discovered the next day, a diagnosis may be impossible.

There are a number of causes of hyperthermia. Older people may succumb to heat during summer months because of an underlying disease which contributes to their inability to cope with heat, or their dwellings may not have an appropriate cooling system. Malignant hyperthermia is a syndrome which develops in people who react to certain drugs, such a phenathiozines(thorazine) or halothane. The use of cocaine and methamphetamine are also associated with hyperthermia. In some of these cases there is a genetic predisposition toward developing "malignant" hyperthermia.

HYPOTHERMIA

Hypothermia occurs more commonly in those individuals who have underlying disease or are incapacitated, such as under the influence of alcohol. People can die from improperly heated homes or apartments or if they are caught outside in the cold. Alcoholics can become hypothermic if they fall asleep in the cold while inebriated. Nursing home patients can succumb to the cold after becoming confused and walking outdoors during winter months.

There are usually no external signs of trauma unless the individual was rendered incapacitated by an injury before dying from the cold.

"Paradoxical undressing" may occur because the individual may begin to undress while dying from the cold. This may appear suspicious if the decedent is a naked woman found outside with her clothes strewn about. An initial impression may suggest sexual assault, but further investigation should uncover the correct manner and cause of death.

FIGURE 11.1 Any sudden death near an electric cord (arrow) must be evaluated for a possible electrocution since there may be no injuries on the body if the death is due to low voltage. Deaths from electrocution occur by electrical charges traveling through the heart, causing arrhythmias, or through the brain, causing an interference with heart and lung functions.

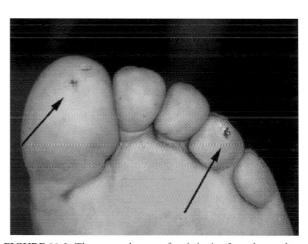

FIGURE 11.2 There may be very few injuries from low voltage deaths; these small lesions are typical and may be easy to miss.

FIGURE 11.3 The only injury to this man who died of electrocution is a burned-off left little finger. This was probably the entrance site. See next photo.

FIGURE 11.4 He was working on this electrical box at his farm. The wires were "hot" and he thought he could work around them safely. See next photo.

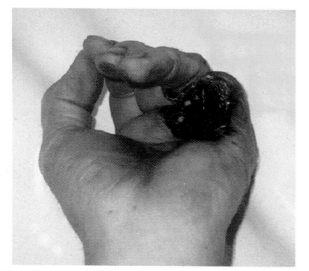

FIGURE 11.5 A closer view of the missing finger. The man died because the charge traveled up through the arm and across his chest into the heart.

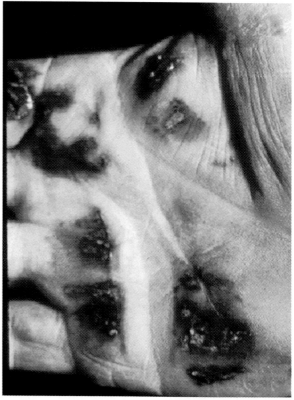

FIGURE 11.6 Entrance burns from grabbing a "hot" wire.

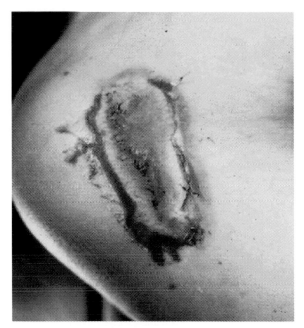

FIGURE 11.7 Burn mark of entrance.

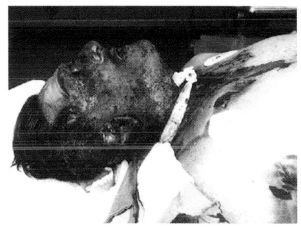

FIGURE 11.9 This man was both electrocuted and burned. He has direct injuries from the electrocution and burns from his clothing. See next photo.

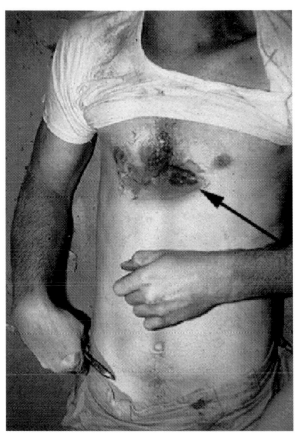

FIGURE 11.8 The arrow points to an outline of the head of pliers the man was holding in his right hand. He was crawling on the ground under a house fixing the wiring when he came into contact with an uninsulated wire. The burn on the chest indicates the path of the charge throughout the heart.

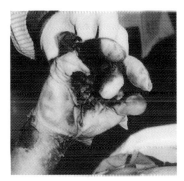

FIGURE 11.11 Another case of skin slippage caused by the heat during an electrocution.

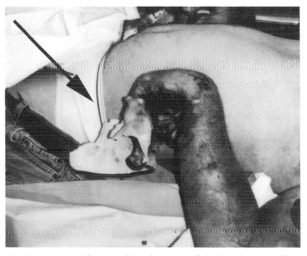

FIGURE 11.10 There is skin slippage of the hands caused by the heat.

FIGURE 11.12 This young man was on his internship with a cable company when he touched a high tension wire (70,000 volts) with some metal rods. See next photo.

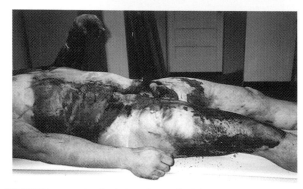

FIGURE 11.13 He had significant flash burns under his clothing from the heat. See next photo.

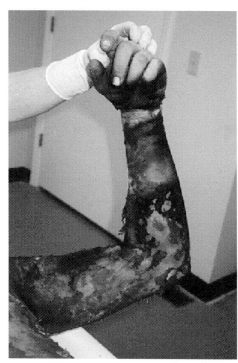

FIGURE 11.14 Flash burns of the arm under the clothing. See next photo.

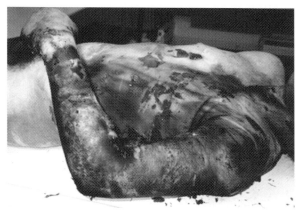

FIGURE 11.15 The burning of the body did not occur in any systematic order. Some parts of the body were not burned. See next photo.

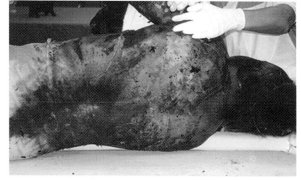

FIGURE 11.16 There was significant injury to the back. See next photo.

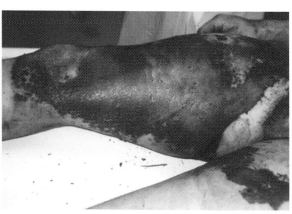

FIGURE 11.17 One leg was much more damaged than the other. See next photo.

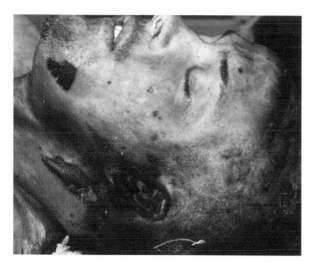

FIGURE 11.18 His left ear was almost completely burned off. This was probably the exit site.

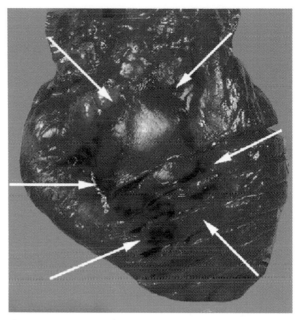

FIGURE 11.19 Direct damage of the heart from burning through the chest wall.

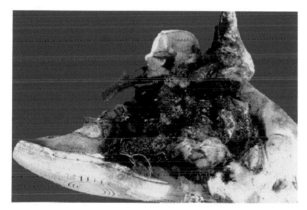

FIGURE 11.20 High voltage electrocutions can cause significant injuries. This foot was burned off when a person stepped on a high voltage wire.

FIGURE 11.22 Many people who die of overdoses do so in squalid living conditions. See next photo.

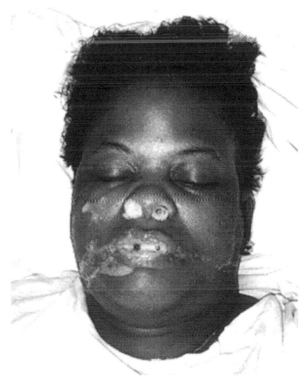

FIGURE 11.21 Drug Abuse. Froth in the nose and mouth is a sign of overdose. However, froth may also occur in drowning victims.

FIGURE 11.23 Examination of the scene usually reveals evidence of drug abuse.

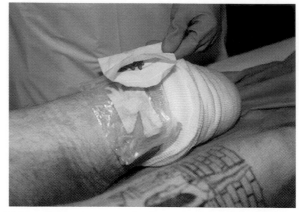

FIGURE 11.24 Drugs can be found in the most unlikely spots. Pills and a syringe were discovered in the bandages of this prisoner's amputation site. Drugs can also be found in the stomach and rectum of carriers (mules).

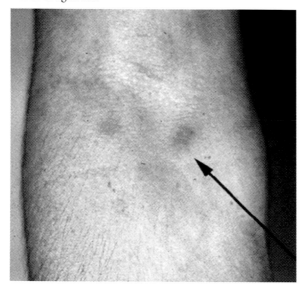

FIGURE 11.25 Hemorrhages in the arms are the most common signs of needle sticks. Of course, this may have been caused during the resuscitation attempt.

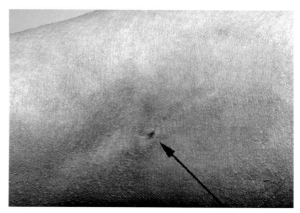

FIGURE 11.26 A needle puncture with surrounding scarring of the skin.

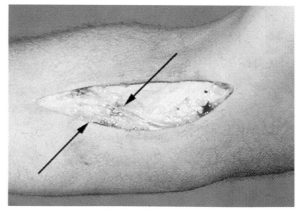

FIGURE 11.28 Incisions into the arm by a pathologist to look for damaged blood vessels. These veins are normal.

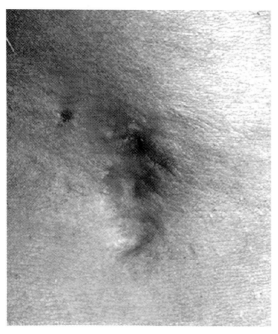

FIGURE 11.27 An area of old (inactive) needle activity in the arm.

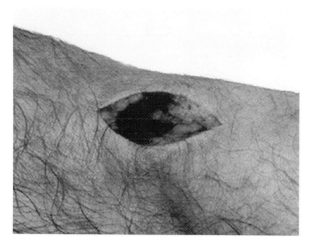

FIGURE 11.29 Hemorrhage in the soft tissues of the arm from a needle puncture.

FIGURE 11.30 Multiple areas of hemorrhage on the arm from recent I.V. use by an addict.

FIGURE 11.31 This decomposed body was discovered under a bridge. The cause of death could not be determined by gross examination at the autopsy. See next photo.

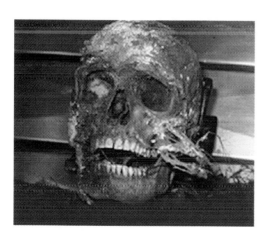

FIGURE 11.32 The brain was decomposed; however, a toxicological photo revealed the presence of an inordinate amount of amitriptyline.

FIGURE 11.33 This lung from an intravenous drug abuser was remarkably heavy and contained thousands of granulomas — the body's reaction from the filler material in the drugs.

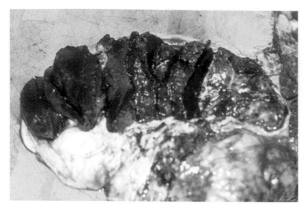

FIGURE 11.34 This stomach contains over 16–20 ounces of charcoal, given as an antidote for drug overdose. Unfortunately, the person died of an unrelated ruptured cerebral aneurysm.

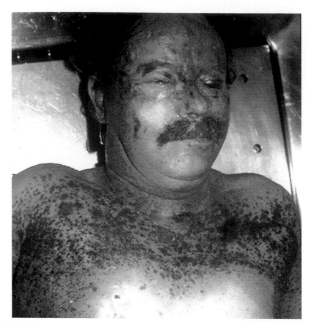

FIGURE 11.35 A person dying of hyperthemia may have no findings other than an unusually quick onset of decomposition. The scene investigation is vitally important. Death due to hyperthermia may be associated with a genetic defect (malignant hyperthemia) and drugs.

FIGURE 11.36 Hypothermia. People caught out in the cold can die. They usually are incapacitated in some fashion (drugs, disease, or trauma) that renders them unconscious. See next photo.

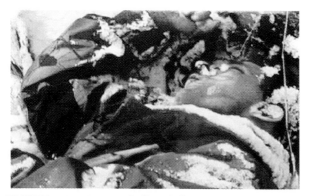

FIGURE 11.37 Autopsy findings in hypothermic cases may be unremarkable or there may be signs of the underlying disease or trauma. Some individuals have areas of bleeding in the stomach lining. Occasionally, individuals will remove their clothing while they are dying of the cold (paradoxical undressing).

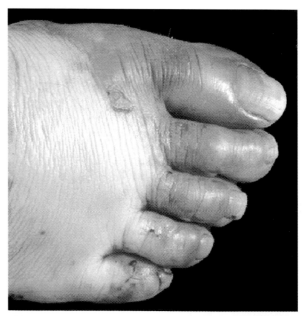

FIGURE 11.38 Frostbite of the toes is only seen in people who have survived for a period of time after the incident. This should not be seen in people who died suddenly from hypothermia.

Chapter 12

CUTTING AND STABBING

CUTTING (INCISED) WOUNDS

An incised wound (cut) is made by a sharp instrument and is longer on the skin surface than it is deep. The edges of the wound are sharp and are usually not ragged or abraded. The surrounding skin is usually undamaged. Within the wound, tissue bridges do not connect one side to the other, as seen in lacerations.

STAB WOUNDS

A stab wound is deeper than it is wide. The size of a skin defect rarely gives an indication of the depth of a stab wound. The ends of the stab wound are the angles. The angles of the wound may be blunt or sharp, depending on the weapon. A single-edged blade will create one blunt angle and one sharp angle. Knives with two cutting surfaces will cause two sharp angles. Home-made sharpened weapons may produce wounds having either sharp or dull angles.

The width and length of a weapon's blade may be determined by analyzing a stab wound. A 0.5"-wide blade, for example, may cause a 0.5"-wide wound on the skin surface if a knife is inserted and removed straight. If either the victim or assailant moves, the external wound may be longer. An external wound may also be slightly shorter because of the skin's elasticity. The depth of the wound track may be longer than the length of the blade because skin and surrounding tissues will collapse and spring back as the pressure is relieved.

GENERAL DISCUSSION

Multiple incised and/or stab wounds of the neck, face, and extremities (so-called "defense" wounds) are usually caused by an assailant. Multiple incised wounds of varying depths on the neck or wrists suggest a suicide. Superficially incised wounds adjacent to a major incised wound are referred to as hesitation marks and are characteristic of self-inflicted injuries. A body sustaining tens or hundreds of stab and incised wounds is characteristic of a situation known as "overkill" which usually occurs in a highly emotional setting such as one involving sex and/or drugs.

FIGURE 12.1 Rarely is the weapon discovered in the wound. Matching the weapon to a wound cannot be done with certainty unless the tip of the blade breaks off and can be matched to the weapon.

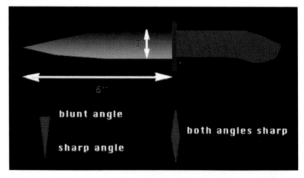

FIGURE 12.2 A single-edged knife with a 6"-long and 1"-wide blade can cause a stab wound 6" or more in depth. A wound this deep will be an inch or more on the outside of the body. The wound will also have one blunt angle and one sharp angle.

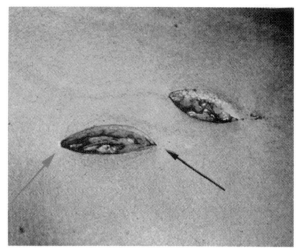

FIGURE 12.3 Stab wounds. The wound on the left has one blunt angle and one sharp angle (darker arrow).

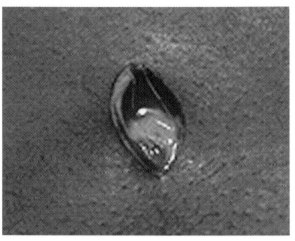

FIGURE 12.4 The skin's elasticity will cause wounds to have different shapes. This wound was caused by a thin blade; however, the wound is rounder due to the skin's elasticity.

FIGURE 12.5 These two stab wounds were caused by the same weapon. The skin was cut around the upper wound causing the wound to look much different than the wound's appearance when first seen.

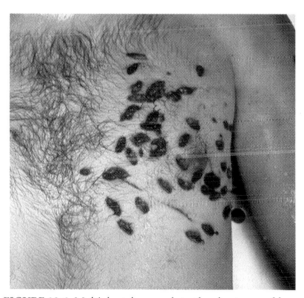

FIGURE 12.6 Multiple stab wounds to the chest, caused by the same knife. This is an "overkill." Drugs and sex must be considered when overkills occur.

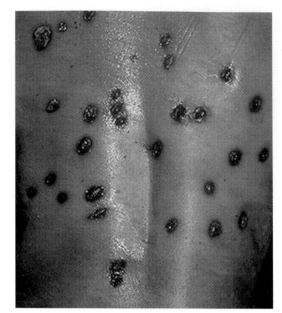

FIGURE 12.7 Wound angles may not be easily evaluated when the wounds dry. The examiner must be conservative when interpreting the angles in such cases.

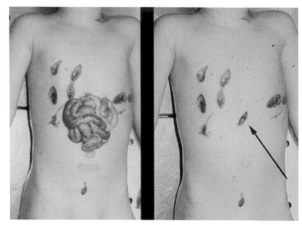

FIGURE 12.8 This child was stabbed multiple times by a drugged uncle. The bowel protruded from one of the wounds of the abdomen (arrow).

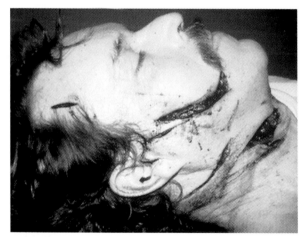

FIGURE 12.9 Multiple incised wounds of the face are considered homicidal. This man received these in a fight in a bar.

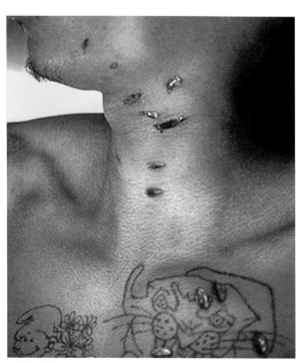

FIGURE 12.10 Multiple stab wounds of the neck and chest. These are homicidal wounds.

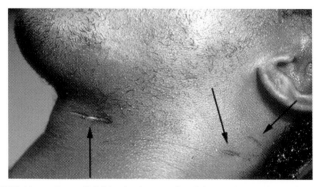

FIGURE 12.11 Superficial incised wounds of the neck may be self-inflicted.

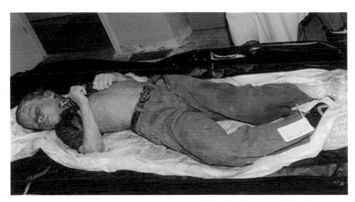

FIGURE 12.12 This boy and the rest of his family were killed by two men. He drowned after his throat was cut and he was thrown into a pond. See next photo.

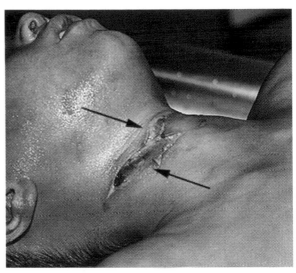

FIGURE 12.13 The boy's neck wounds were superficial and did not contribute to death.

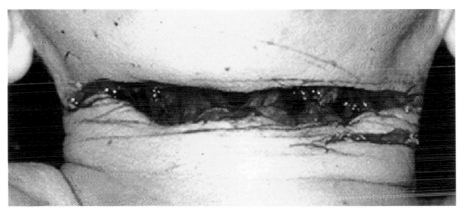

FIGURE 12.14 Deep incised wounds to the neck may be either suicidal or homicidal. In this case, the multiple superficial incised wounds (hesitation marks) are signs of a suicide.

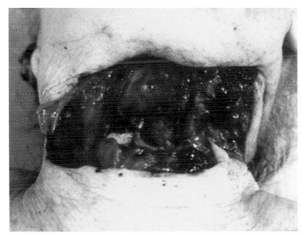

FIGURE 12.15 Deep incised wounds of the neck. There are no hesitation marks. This was a homicide.

FIGURE 12.16 This woman was talking on the phone with her mother when a man entered her apartment and killed her. See next photo.

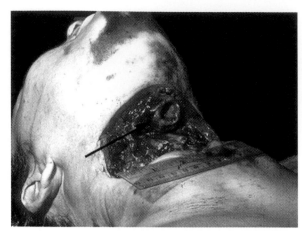

FIGURE 12.17 Her windpipe (larynx) was severed, causing her to suffocate. Few blood vessels were cut. The abrasions on her chin are "rug burns." See next photo.

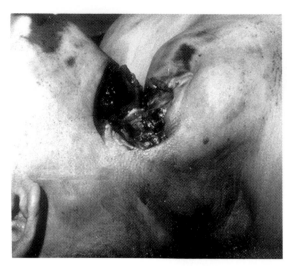

FIGURE 12.18 A side view reveals the clean deep cuts with no hesitation marks.

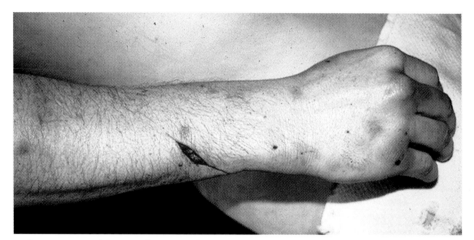

FIGURE 12.19 This incised wound of the arm occurred when the decedent raised his arm in a defensive posture.

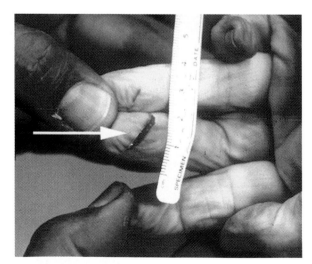

FIGURE 12.20 Incised wounds to the fingers from grabbing the assailant's knife.

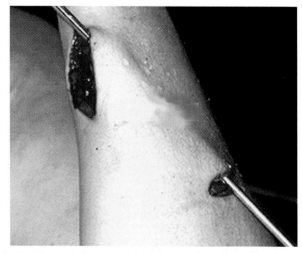

FIGURE 12.21 Stab wound of the arm from defending herself. The entrance is on the lower right.

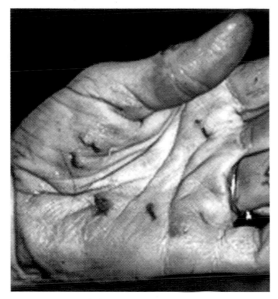

FIGURE 12.22 Multiple stab wounds of the hand, caused by a screwdriver.

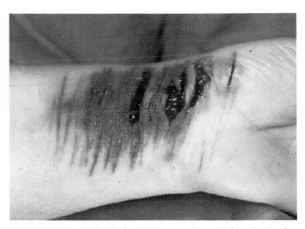

FIGURE 12.23 Multiple hesitation marks and deep incised wounds in this suicide. The cause of death was from cutting the neck.

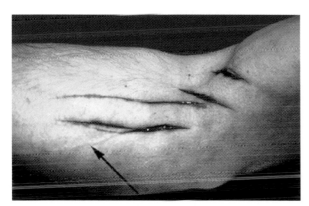

FIGURE 12.24 Suicide attempt. The cuts to the arm went in the wrong direction. The decedent decided to hang himself when the knife didn't work. The arrow points to an old scar from a previous attempt.

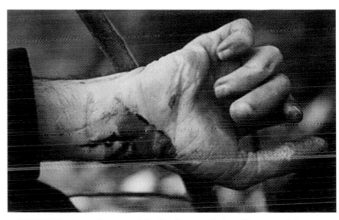

FIGURE 12.25 Scars and incised wounds in a "jumper." See next photo.

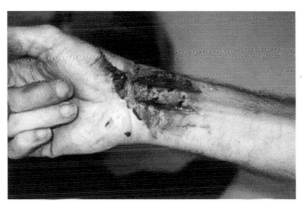

FIGURE 12.26 The other arm also had recent cuts.

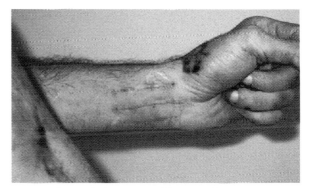

FIGURE 12.27 Obvious scars of the wrist from a previous suicide attempt.

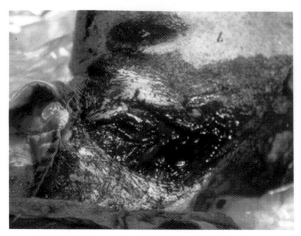

FIGURE 12.28 Incised wound of the neck from a chainsaw. The man was trimming a tree when the chainsaw kicked back into his neck.

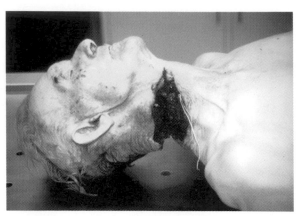

FIGURE 12.29 Incised wound of the neck, caused by a saw. See next photo.

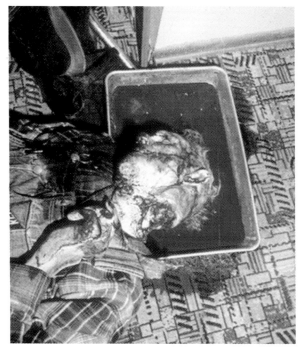

FIGURE 12.30 The man was killed by blunt trauma to the head by his stepson. The stepson attempted to cut off the head in order to find the "microfilm" in his stepfather's head. Notice the head was placed over a pan to keep from making a mess. See next photo.

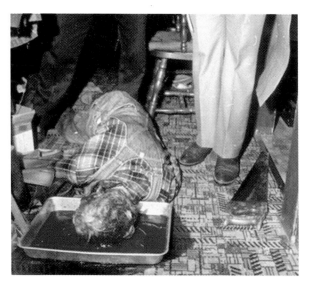

FIGURE 12.31 Another view, showing the saw. The stepson confessed to the crime and stated he stopped sawing after he became tired.

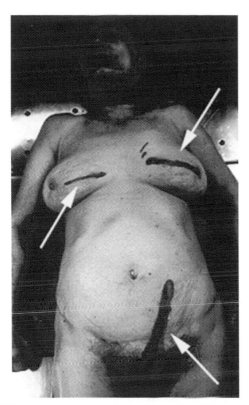

FIGURE 12.32 Postmortem incised wounds of the genitalia and breasts.

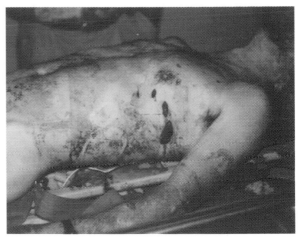

FIGURE 12.33 Physicians may alter the appearance of wounds or add new ones to the body during resuscitation attempts. This man was stabbed to death. Two of the wounds are thoracotomy incisions to drain blood from the chest. See next photo.

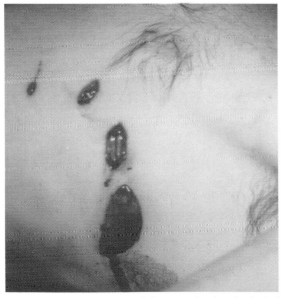

FIGURE 12.34 A closer view of the wounds after the body has been cleaned. The upper wounds were caused by an assailant and the lower two were caused by a physician in the ER.

FIGURE 12.35 This 14-year-old girl was killed while she was taking a nap in her bed. This is the entire crime scene. A knife was left in her face above the eye (arrow). See next photo.

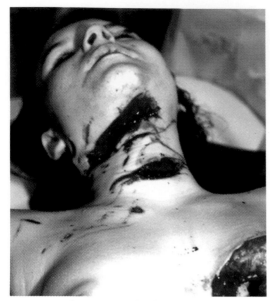

FIGURE 12.36 There were multiple incised and stab wounds of the neck, trunk, and extremities. See next photo.

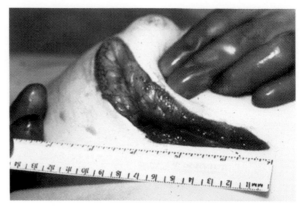

FIGURE 12.37 There was a large defect in the chest with more than one stab wound. See next photo.

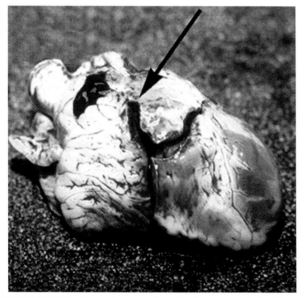

FIGURE 12.38 The stab wounds to the heart revealed a blunt angle (arrow). Some organs such as the heart and the liver may give better views of the angles than the outside of the body. See next photo.

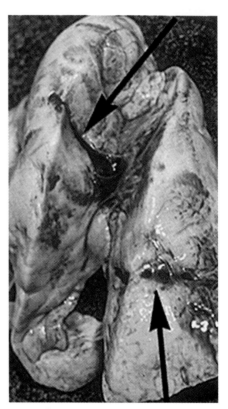

FIGURE 12.39 There were multiple stab wounds in the left lung. See next photo.

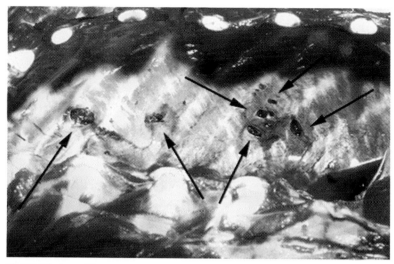

FIGURE 12.40 The arrows point to some of the ten stab wounds to the inside left chest wall. The victim was stabbed at least ten times through the single large wound of the chest.

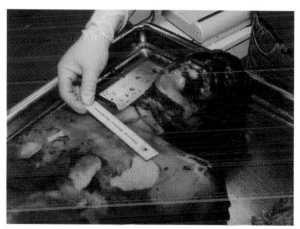

FIGURE 12.41 This man received at least seven incised wounds to the neck prior to being struck in the head with a brick. His body was then burned in his trailer. See next photo.

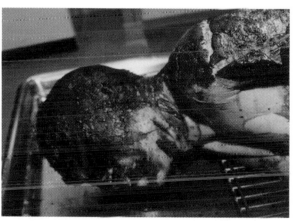

FIGURE 12.42 Closer view of the incised wounds made prior to the thermal injury.

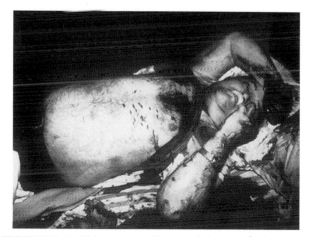

FIGURE 12.43 This man was discovered dead on the bed in his apartment. See next photo.

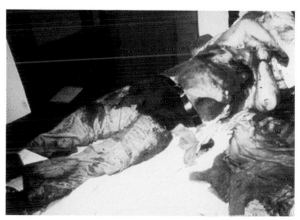

FIGURE 12.44 Numerous stab wounds of the chest were seen at the scene. See next photo.

FIGURE 12.45 There was blood on beer bottles. See next photo.

FIGURE 12.46 Little was in the refrigerator except for an empty six-pack container and blood. See next photo.

FIGURE 12.47 In the bathroom, there was blood on the stool. See next photo.

FIGURE 12.48 Blood was on the tub. See next photo.

FIGURE 12.49 Abundant blood was on the walls and sink. See next photo.

FIGURE 12.50 A closer view of the sink. Notice the knife. See next photo.

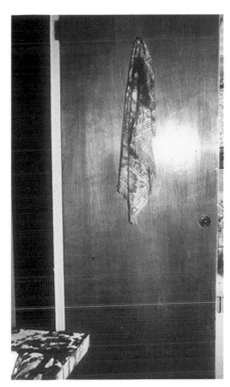

FIGURE 12.51 A towel with blood hung on the door. See next photo.

FIGURE 12.52 A bloody footprint was present on the closet floor. It was measured. See next photo.

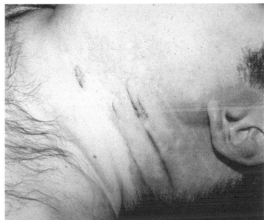

FIGURE 12.53 Examination of the neck at the morgue revealed superficial incised wounds of the neck. See next photo.

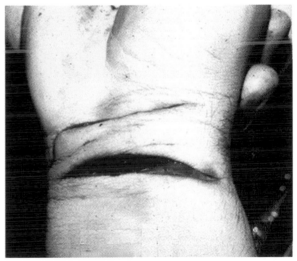

FIGURE 12.54 Deep and superficial wounds of the wrist. See next photo.

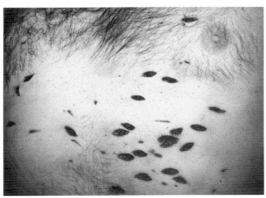

FIGURE 12.55 Only two of the stab wounds to the chest penetrated vital organs. This was a suicide. The man drank some beer, took a shower, went to the bathroom, and finally died in his bed. The bloody footprint discovered in the closet was his.

— Chapter 13 —

MOTOR VEHICLE INJURIES

OCCUPANTS

When a motor vehicle is involved in an accident, the driver and passenger's bodies react as if they travel toward the site of the impact. For example, an impact to the front left of a car during a head-on crash will cause occupants to have injuries on their left, especially if unrestrained. The driver may hit the steering wheel, dashboard, or windshield, and the passenger the dashboard, windshield, or rearview mirror. Each may have significant injuries even though they hit different objects.

There may be few external marks when there are seat belts and airbags; internally, however, there may be impressive injuries to the heart and aorta. Seat belt abrasions on the shoulder and hips are common. The location of the marks helps differentiate between the driver and the passenger.

Side window glass causes a characteristic injury because it is made of tempered glass which will shatter into numerous small fragments upon impact. These fragments will cause a characteristic "dicing" pattern of lacerated-abrasions on the face, shoulders, or arms. A driver will have dicing injuries on the left side of the body and a passenger will have them on the right.

Other common injuries involve fractures of the patella (knee), femurs and ankles caused by hitting the dashboard and the extremities caught under the seat. High-speed collisions can cause multiple severe injuries. There may be extensive skull fractures and facial lacerations, contusions, and abrasions. Common injuries to the trunk include rib and pelvic fractures with associated internal injuries. Lacerations of these internal organs may occur without associated rib fractures. If any of the occupants are ejected during a crash, obviously the injuries may be quite variable and very severe. Head trauma is common in these situations. In addition, when an occupant is ejected, a vehicle may roll over and compress the occupants, causing compressive asphyxia, often with few other injuries.

Motorcyclists usually die from head trauma. Helmets may or may not prevent serious injury, depending on the force of the impact. They may also have numerous injuries similar to pedestrians because they are so often launched unrestrained to impact with the ground or other objects.

PEDESTRIANS

In a hit-and-run fatality, a study of the injuries may help identify the vehicle. The points of impact on a body are particularly important and clothing must be closely examined for paint chips and parts of the vehicle that may be transferred on impact. Bumper impact sites on the legs should be measured from the heel. This may indicate the bumper height. A bumper fracture is often triangular in shape with the apex of the triangle pointing in the direction that a vehicle was moving. If a driver applied brakes suddenly, a bumper fracture may be lower than expected because applying the brakes may drop the front end of the car. Adults tend to be run under while children with a lower center of gravity tend to be run over.

FIGURE 13.1 Major accidents may or may not have associated deaths. Two people died in this head-on collision.

FIGURE 13.2 The examiner or investigator should know the position of the decedent in the vehicle.

FIGURE 13.3 This woman was lying outside the car. Was she in this position when first discovered? The investigator must speak with the first people to arrive at the scene.

FIGURE 13.4 Careful examination of the vehicle may reveal areas on or in the car where the occupant made contact. There is brain material in this door frame.

FIGURE 13.5 Leather sole shoes may have impressions from the brake or accelerator pedals. This may give a clue as to how the driver was reacting at the time of the accident.

FIGURE 13.6 This vehicle ran straight into a tree. This was a suicide. The driver also had incised wounds of one of his wrists.

FIGURE 13.7 The driver of this car drove his vehicle into a rock wall. A suicide note was discovered in the trunk.

FIGURE 13.8 This woman was dead at the scene. The airbag prevented any external injuries.

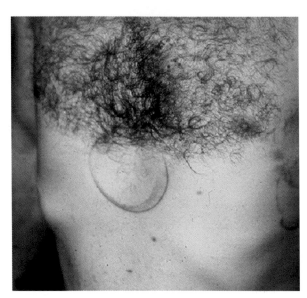

FIGURE 13.9 This is not an injury from the steering wheel. It is an abrasion from shocking the decedent during CPR. Notice similar marks on the left side of the chest.

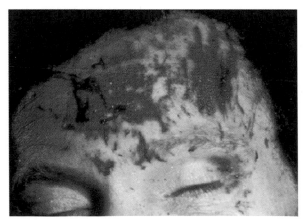

FIGURE 13.10 This man's forehead is abraded and torn from an impact with the windshield.

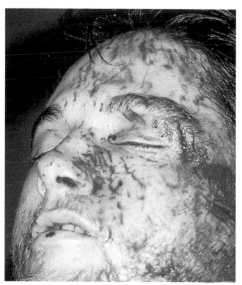

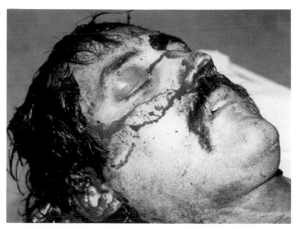

FIGURE 13.12 The black eyes (spectacle hemorrhages) were caused by blood seeping down into the face from fractures of the skull above the eyes.

FIGURE 13.11 The angulated cuts on this man's face were caused by contact with the side window. The tempered glass making up the side window fractures in cubes. These injuries are called "dicing abrasions."

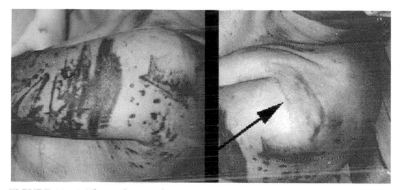

FIGURE 13.13 These photos of an occupant reveal injuries to the shoulder and upper arm. The arrow points to the mark made by a seat belt, proving the decedent was the driver.

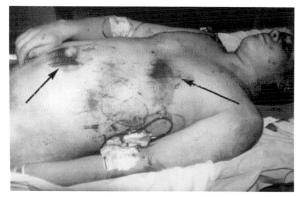

FIGURE 13.14 Occupants may receive many different kinds of injuries. The arrow on the left points to a distinct pattern that could not be matched to any particular point in the car.

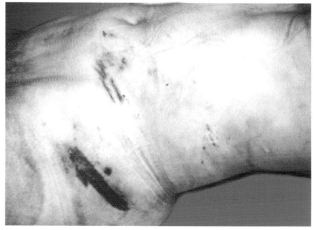

FIGURE 13.15 The mark on this woman's hip is from the lap belt.

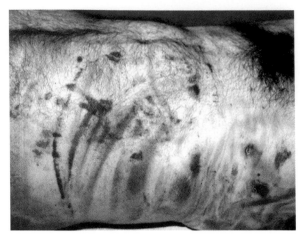

FIGURE 13.16 Many nonspecific external injuries may be evident on an occupant.

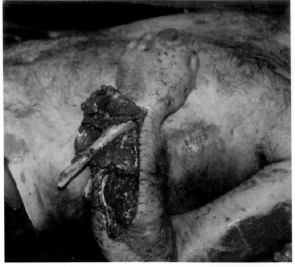

FIGURE 13.17 Extremity fractures with lacerations in a driver.

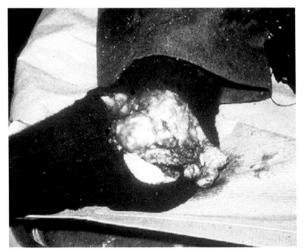

FIGURE 13.18 This open fracture of the ankle occurred when the driver's foot was caught under the seat.

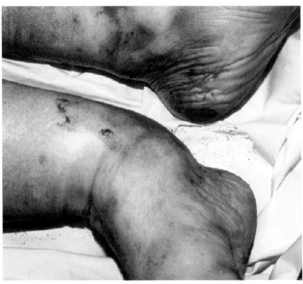

FIGURE 13.19 Closed fractures of the ankles.

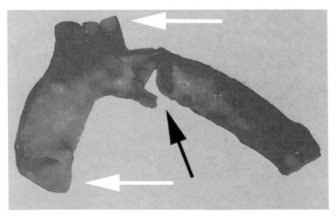

FIGURE 13.20 The black arrow points to the most common site for aortic rupture during a chest impact. The lower white arrow points to the end of the aorta which attaches to the heart. This area may also rupture.

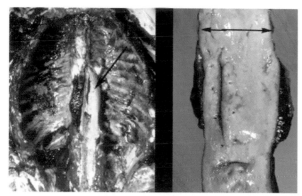

FIGURE 13.21 This is an unusual tear in the aorta. The tear is usually horizontal (arrow on right) and not vertical as in this case.

FIGURE 13.22 Extensive lacerations of the liver from an impact with the abdomen and lower chest.

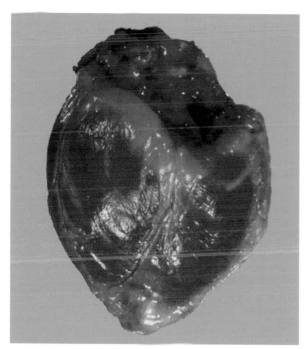

FIGURE 13.23 This heart was completely torn off and discovered floating in the left chest cavity.

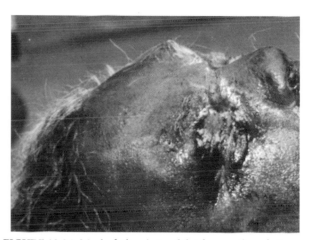

FIGURE 13.24 Marked abrasions of the face are from being thrown around inside the vehicle.

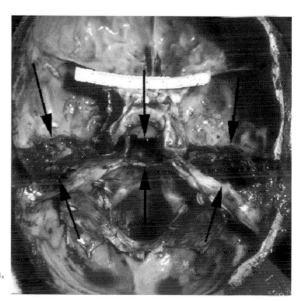

FIGURE 13.25 A hinged fracture of the skull. On external examination, blood would be present in the decedent's ear canals.

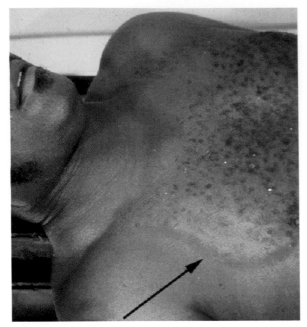

FIGURE 13.26 The only mark on this man's body was this contusion from a truck's cab, which trapped him as the truck trapped him. The man attempted to jump clear of the truck as it began to roll over. He died of asphyxiation.

FIGURE 13.27 In this accident, the car overturned and one of the passengers was discovered dead, lying in this position. See next photo.

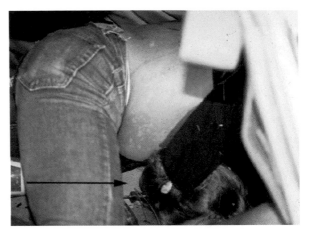

FIGURE 13.28 A closer view reveals the boy's head (arrow) tightly compressed against his chest. He died from positional asphyxiation.

FIGURE 13.29 Pedestrians may receive injuries from striking the vehicle after being thrown into the air. There may also be secondary impact sites on the vehicles.

FIGURE 13.30 Adult pedestrians tend to be "run under" when struck by automobiles. This man was struck and lifted into the air, coming to rest on the car's top and windshield. See next photo.

FIGURE 13.31 A closer view of the body's final resting position.

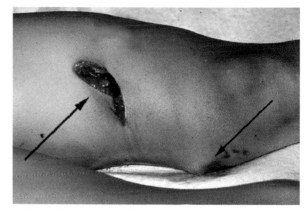

FIGURE 13.32 Fractured bones may not match the external sites of impact.

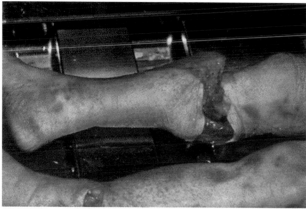

FIGURE 13.33 The heights of fractures need to be measured. The fracture heights may be matched to bumper heights. The distances may indicate whether or not the vehicle was braking at the time of impact.

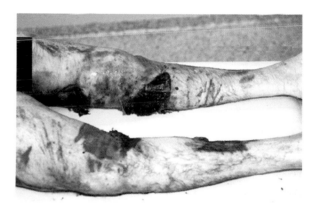

FIGURE 13.34 Multiple points of impact from being struck during a hit-and-run.

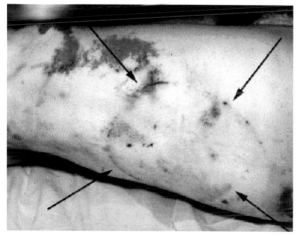

FIGURE 13.35 Patterns from the vehicle may be found. The arrows outline a headlight on this man's leg.

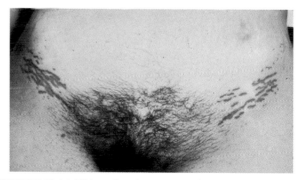

FIGURE 13.36 This pedestrian was struck in the back. The marks on her body are stretch marks.

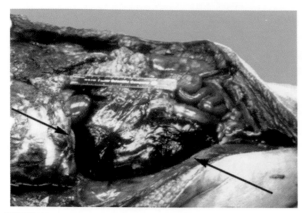

FIGURE 13.37 Retroperitoneal hemorrhage. This state trooper was struck by a drunk driver's car while issuing a ticket to another drunk driver.

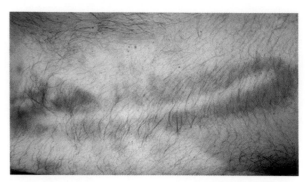

FIGURE 13.38 This pedestrian was struck by a truck. Paint chips on the clothing and this mark with the pale center on his leg helped to identify the particular type of truck.

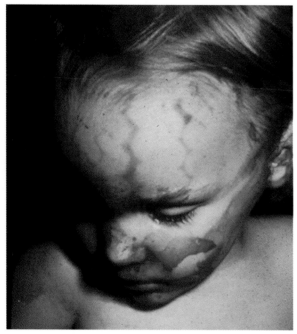

FIGURE 13.39 The tread pattern on the child's head may be matched to the vehicle that struck him.

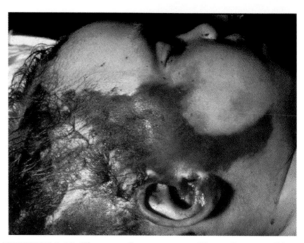

FIGURE 13.40 These marks were caused by a tire, stretching the skin.

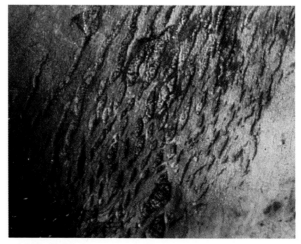

FIGURE 13.41 Stretch marks from a tire.

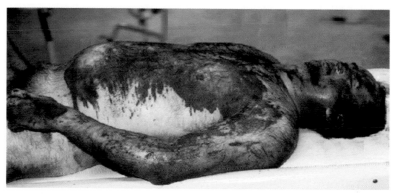

FIGURE 13.42 This is an example of "road rash" after the man was ejected from the vehicle and slid across the road.

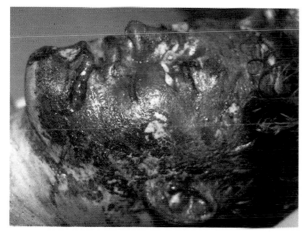

FIGURE 13.43 Road rash of the face.

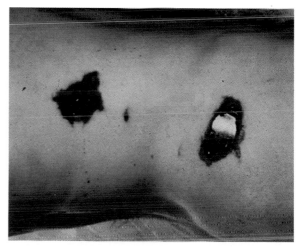

FIGURE 13.44 Pieces of the vehicle may be embedded in the body.

FIGURE 13.45 Pieces of paint and other material found on clothing are important to collect. They may be matched to missing areas on a vehicle, as in this case.

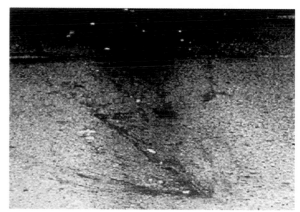

FIGURE 13.46 After high speed impacts, the site of initial impact may be quite some distance from the body.

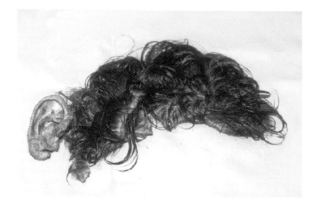

FIGURE 13.47 This scalp with ear was discovered on the truck involved in a hit-and-run.

FIGURE 13.48 This boy was decapitated after a hit-and-run. The distance of the head from the body helped prove the speed of the car. See next photo.

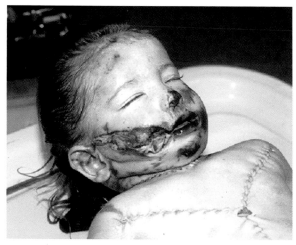

FIGURE 13.49 The boy's head was reattached and there was an open casket funeral.

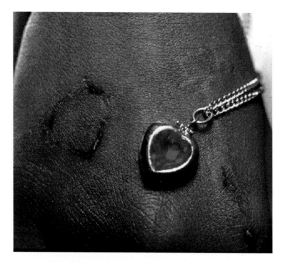

FIGURE 13.50 The girl wearing this bracelet was struck with such force that the bracelet abraded the skin.

FIGURE 13.51 Motorcycles can be dangerous. Most fatalities occur because of head trauma. See next photo.

FIGURE 13.52 The body was thrown free of the motorcycle and impacted against the ground.

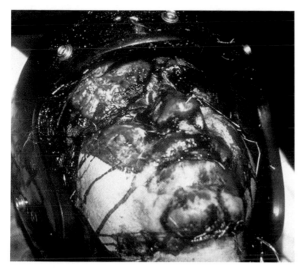

FIGURE 13.53 Most motorcyclists die from head trauma even if they are wearing helmets.

FIGURE 13.54 This accident did not appear serious; even so, the driver was dead. See next photo.

FIGURE 13.55 There was no damage to the vehicle or apparent injury to the driver. Autopsy revealed he died of a heart attack. When accidents are minor and the driver is dead, the investigator must think of a natural cause first.

FIGURE 13.56 This was the scene of a head-on collision. See next photo.

FIGURE 13.57 The driver's wife, sitting on the passenger side, only had a broken arm.

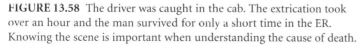

FIGURE 13.58 The driver was caught in the cab. The extrication took over an hour and the man survived for only a short time in the ER. Knowing the scene is important when understanding the cause of death.

FIGURE 13.59 This airplane was pulled from the river after the pilot lost control. See next photo.

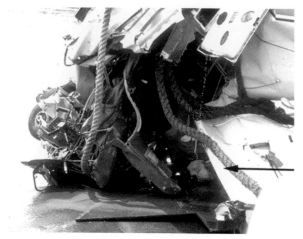

FIGURE 13.60 The pilot was still pinned in the wreckage (arrow).

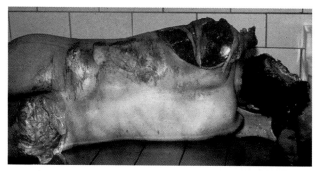

FIGURE 13.61 These extensive cutting injuries were caused by the propeller of an airplane. This man worked at the airport and walked in front of a small plane.

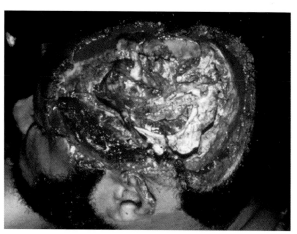

FIGURE 13.62 The propeller sliced off much of the side of his head.

FIGURE 13.63 These are the remains of a man who died in an airplane accident. The body was so badly distorted that it could not be positively identified.

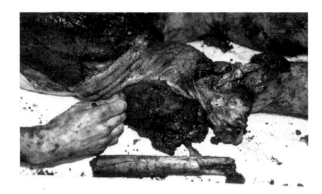

FIGURE 13.64 Train accidents can cause marked injuries and distortion of the body.

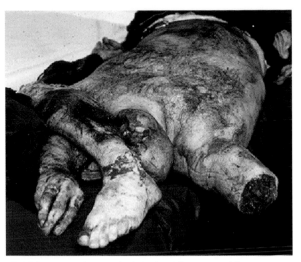

FIGURE 13.65 More train injuries. The extremities appear as if they have been neatly incised.

FIGURE 13.66 This young man was racing his motorcycle over a hill when he came down hard against the handlebars. See next photo.

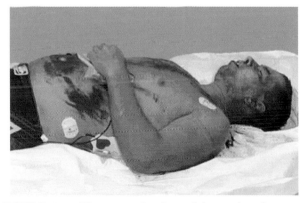

FIGURE 13.67 There were abrasions of the trunk and no other obvious abnormalities. See next photo.

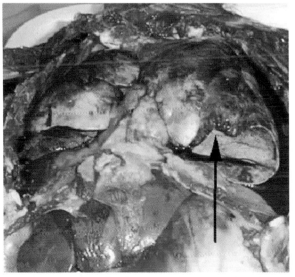

FIGURE 13.68 Internally, there was a laceration of the lung (arrow) and the heart (not shown). See next photo.

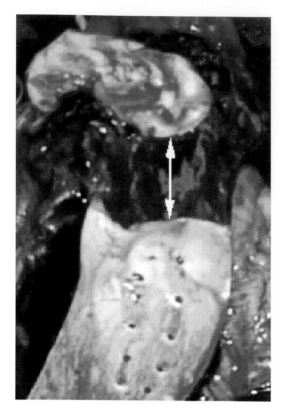

FIGURE 13.69 The most important injury was a transected aorta.

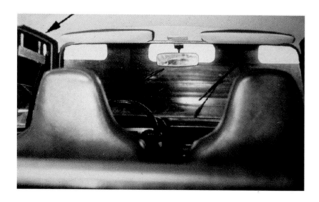

FIGURE 13.71 The car came to rest in the adjacent field and the driver was dead in the front seat. The arrow points to a ruler which is measuring the size of the open window. The driver's hat was discovered next to a fence at the point of initial impact. See next photo.

FIGURE 13.70 A car left the right side of the roadway at this curve. See next photo.

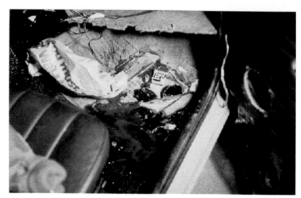

FIGURE 13.72 The driver's head was down below the passenger seat. This was the only area of blood in the car. See next photo.

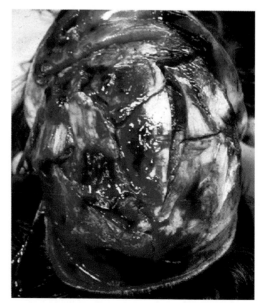

FIGURE 13.73 The driver had multiple skull fractures and an open laceration of the scalp from a frontal impact; however, there were no points of impact(s) present inside the car.

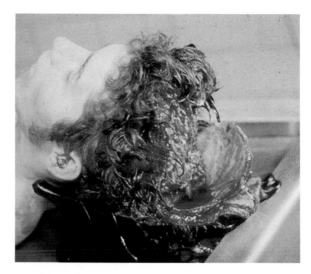

FIGURE 13.74 This driver had an open defect of the skull with impressive brain trauma. See next photo.

FIGURE 13.75 A boy was riding his bicycle at home after work one night. The back wheel of the bicycle revealed he was struck from behind. The body was not at the scene of initial impact. See next photo.

FIGURE 13.76 The body was discovered approximately three miles from the site of the accident. The line of blood next to the body could be followed for two and a half miles. See next photo.

FIGURE 13.77 There were considerable injuries on his side from being dragged. See next photo.

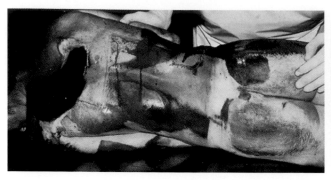

FIGURE 13.78 There were black rubbing marks from the tires of the truck. The only significant injuries to the body were those from being dragged. See next photo.

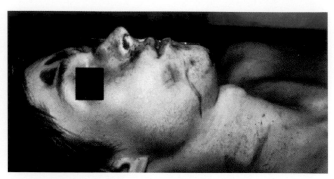

FIGURE 13.79 There were abrasions of the face; however, there was no head trauma. See next photo.

FIGURE 13.80 The truck was discovered in a trailer park. The owner was inside. See next photo.

FIGURE 13.81 There were signs where the bike was struck by the front of the truck. See next photo.

FIGURE 13.82 The driver's shoes were in the sink. He had attempted to wash them. Blood on the shoes matched the decedent's. The driver had no license and had been convicted three times for drunk driving. He was sent to jail for 25 years.

Chapter 14

PEDIATRIC FORENSIC PATHOLOGY

Investigation of fatalities in children requires special expertise because injuries in children may be different and more subtle than those of adults. Children who are repeatedly battered may present with multiple types and ages of injuries. Some may have no visible external injuries but have fatal organ damage internally, such as a ruptured liver. There may be few or no injuries to the head, as in the case of a baby who is violently shaken.

Essential to a correct diagnosis in all infant deaths is the history. The medical personnel who first see these children and interact with the families have the best opportunity to find out from the caregiver what occurred. All statements should be recorded shortly after they have been made. Frequently, the history of how an injury occurred is inconsistent with the pattern and type of injury discovered by the pathologist.

BATTERED CHILD SYNDROME

These children have a history of being repeatedly beaten by a caregiver. The injuries occur over a period of weeks, months, or years. Usually there are numerous injuries of different ages. It is common to see a child with healing rib fractures and old contusions in addition to the recent injuries which caused death. The external injuries to the head from blunt trauma may only be visible on the undersurface of the scalp. Contusions of the trunk may be readily apparent or absent even though there are fatal injuries to the internal organs. All injuries should be photographed.

SHAKEN BABY

Shaking a child or an infant may cause a fatal head injury without external marks. Violent shaking may cause nerve damage, brain swelling, and slight bleeding on and over the brain. Retinal hemorrhages may also occur, but these can only be seen with an ophthalmoscope unless the eyes are removed at autopsy. There may

be contusions on the arms or chest where the infant was grabbed while being shaken. Other blunt impact injuries are often present.

A child usually becomes unconscious or noticeably abnormal within minutes of the violent act. Since there may be no obvious signs of abuse, emergency room personnel may not be suspicious of any foul play. An investigation should be conducted on any child who is dead on arrival or dies in the emergency room. If a child dies in an emergency room, the scene of injury should be visited and investigated.

NEGLECT

Children do not need to be battered with multiple internal and external injuries for a medical examiner to rule a death a homicide. Child abuse and death can result from neglect. For example, if a child is not fed or if a child is left in a harmful situation (like a hot car), death may occur.

If a child is malnourished, his skin may be lax with little underlying soft tissue. He may appear underweight for his age, and the eyes may appear sunken. Vitreous humor (eye fluid) can be sampled and tested for chemical confirmation of dehydration. Sudden loss of weight can be determined by reviewing any previous medical records and comparing past to present weights.

SUDDEN INFANT DEATH SYNDROME (CRIB DEATH)

A diagnosis of SIDS requires a complete autopsy and scene investigation. The diagnosis can only be made if both the scene and the autopsy are negative or unremarkable. There is no probable cause of death. There may be minor injuries to the external body by CPR and insects (anthropophagia); these must not be confused with injuries.

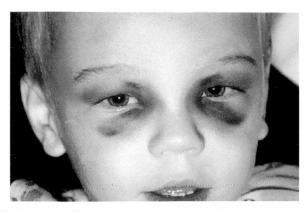

FIGURE 14.1 These spectacle hemorrhages (raccoon's eyes) were caused by blows to the side of the head. There do not have to be fractures of the skull to have spectacle hemorrhages.

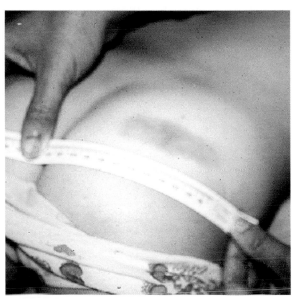

FIGURE 14.2 Injuries must be explained. Not all injuries are due to abuse, but the examiner must be suspicious. This contusion was caused by a belt.

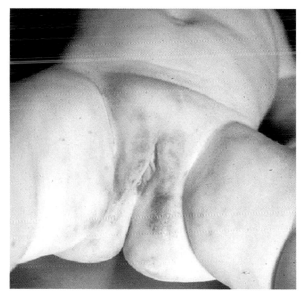

FIGURE 14.3 The lesions on this infant girl suggest abuse; however, there is no injury, only a rash. See next photo.

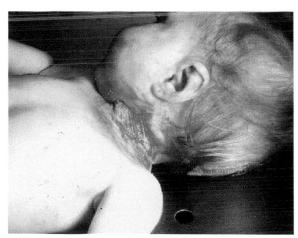

FIGURE 14.4 There was also a rash and infection of the neck. The child died of the infection. The parents did not give the child medicine as prescribed by the physician. This may have been neglect, but not abuse.

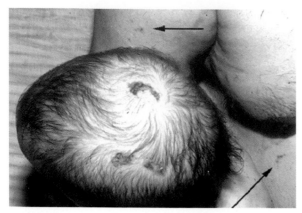

FIGURE 14.5 Notice the lesions on this child's head are similar to the lesions on the father's arm and body (arrows). They are caused by infections. See next photo.

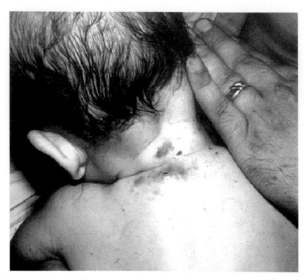

FIGURE 14.6 There were also infected areas on the back and neck.

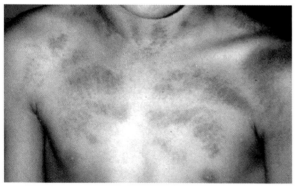

FIGURE 14.7 This child died of an infection. The marks were caused by coin rubbing and not abuse.

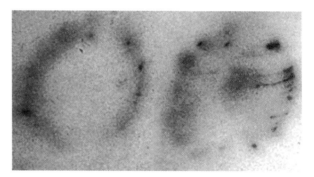

FIGURE 14.8 Bite marks. These should be recognized and measured, as well as swabbed for DNA testing.

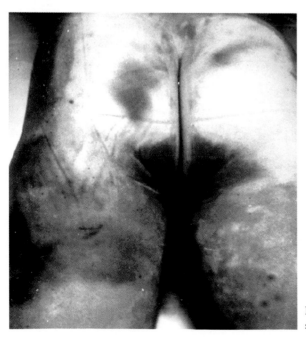

FIGURE 14.9 The buttocks and upper legs of this young boy are extensively contused. These injuries could not have occurred accidentally.

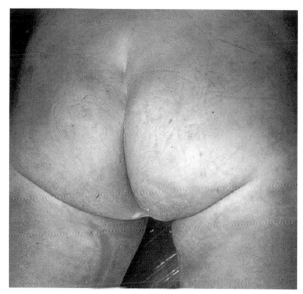

FIGURE 14.10 Blunt trauma to the buttocks may not be easily detected. Incisions into the buttocks should be performed to adequately evaluate the degree of trauma. See next photo.

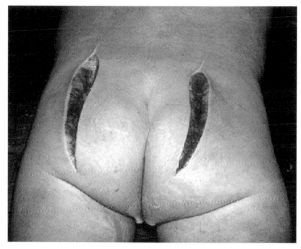

FIGURE 14.11 The buttocks were incised and blood in the soft tissues revealed. Microscopic sections may be helpful in determining the age of the trauma.

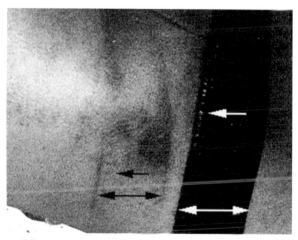

FIGURE 14.13 This belt made the marks on the body. The width and thread marks from the belt match the pattern on the skin (arrows).

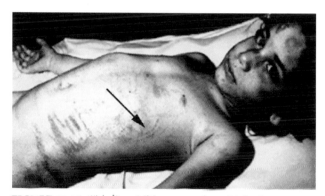

FIGURE 14.12 This live child was struck multiple times over the chest and abdomen. There is a pattern of a shoe print on her left chest.

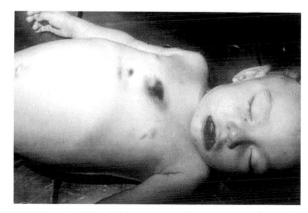

FIGURE 14.14 This child came in with an unusual abraded contusion on his chest. See next photo.

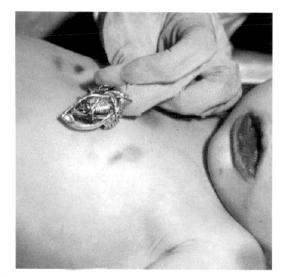

FIGURE 14.15 This silver pendant caused the bruises.

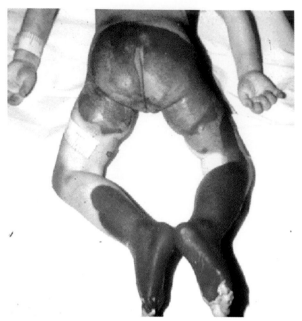

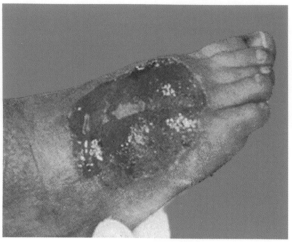

FIGURE 14.17 The lesion was caused by either extreme heat or cold. The child died of head trauma.

FIGURE 14.16 The burn on this girl's buttock was caused by placing her on a stove as punishment for a minor offense.

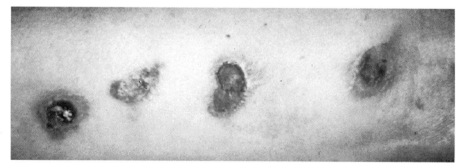

FIGURE 14.18 These are cigarette burns of the arm.

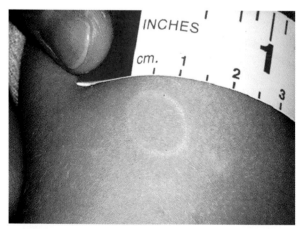

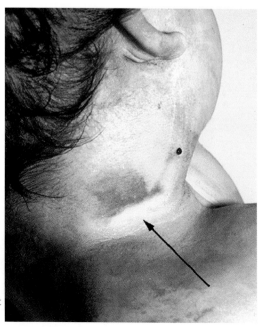

FIGURE 14.19 The circular mark is a healed non-natural lesion which may be a sign of an intentional act of abuse.

FIGURE 14.20 The mark on the neck was caused by a strap from a car seat used to strangle the child.

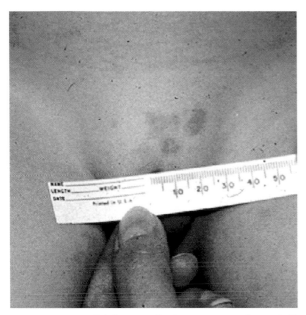

FIGURE 14.21 Multiple recent bruises at or near the genitalia are considered sexual abuse unless there is a compelling story to account for these injuries.

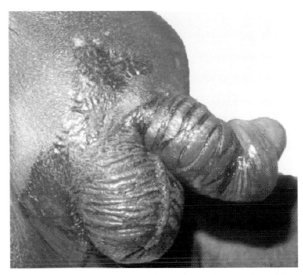

FIGURE 14.22 The scarring and resultant abnormal positioning of the penis is a sign of sexual abuse.

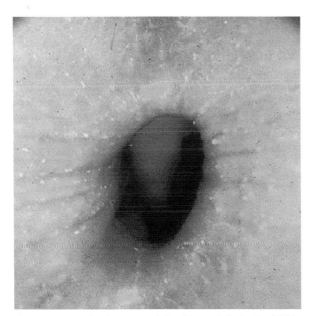

FIGURE 14.23 The firmness of the skin and the lack of folds around the anal opening is a sign of repeated sexual abuse.

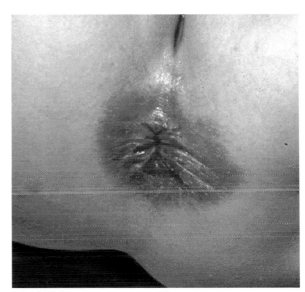

FIGURE 14.24 The rectum has a reddened and reactive surface caused by sodomy.

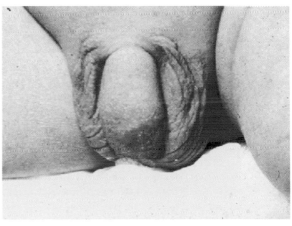

FIGURE 14.25 Bruises on the genitalia of a very young child suggest child abuse.

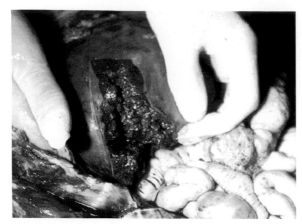

FIGURE 14.26 This laceration of the liver was caused by a blow to the abdomen. There were no external signs of injury.

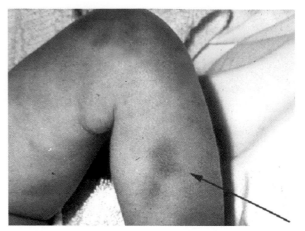

FIGURE 14.27 Children learning to walk may have bruises on their lower legs. The child in this photograph was too young to walk. A bruise on his leg must be viewed with suspicion. An X-ray of the extremity is necessary to rule out a fracture.

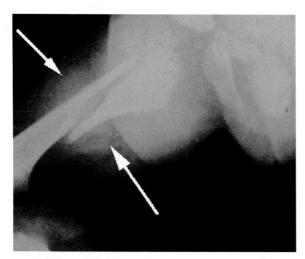

FIGURE 14.28 A fracture in a young child who cannot walk is suggestive of abuse, especially if the fracture is a spiral one as in this case. This type of fracture suggests the leg was twisted.

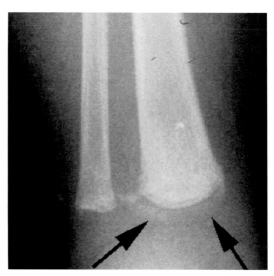

FIGURE 14.30 The fracture site is easier to locate after one week of healing.

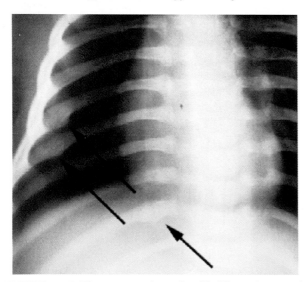

FIGURE 14.29 The arrows point to "puff ball" type lesions of healing rib fractures. Posterior rib fractures are almost always the result of abuse.

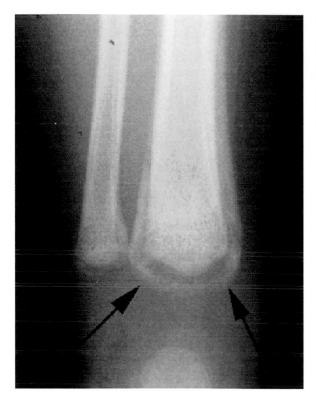

FIGURE 14.31 This tibia has recent fractures on the end of the bone. The fracture sites are difficult to see. See next photo.

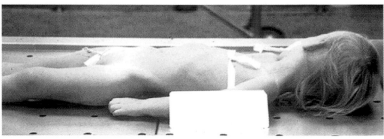

FIGURE 14.32 This child had no external injuries. The mother's boyfriend said the child fell off a table. See next photo.

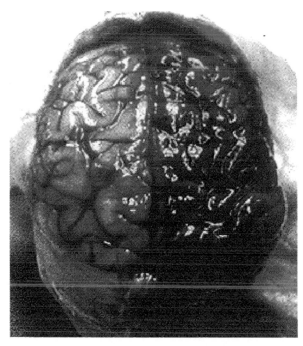

FIGURE 14.33 There was a superficial unilateral subdural hemorrhage over the right side of the brain. This finding and the discovery of retinal hemorrhages confirmed the diagnosis of shaken baby. See next photo.

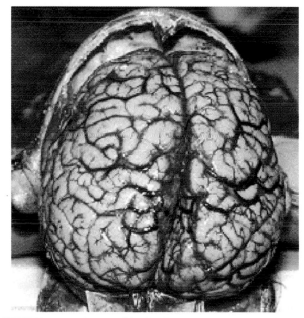

FIGURE 14.34 A normal brain. Compare to previous photo.

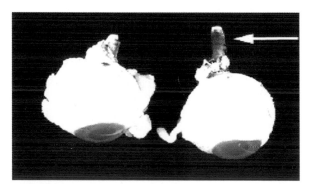

FIGURE 14.35 There were retinal hemorrhages and hemorrhages around the otic nerves (arrow).

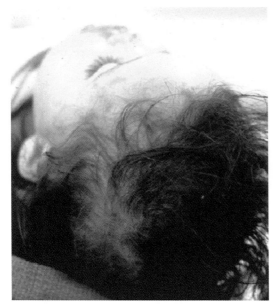

FIGURE 14.36 There were no external injuries in this child, who reportedly fell off the washing machine and struck her head on the floor. External injuries may not be apparent in cases of fatal head trauma. See next photo.

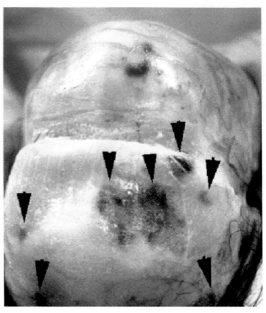

FIGURE 14.37 The story did not fit the findings of multiple subscalpular hemorrhages (arrows). When confronted, the caretaker admitted striking the child numerous times.

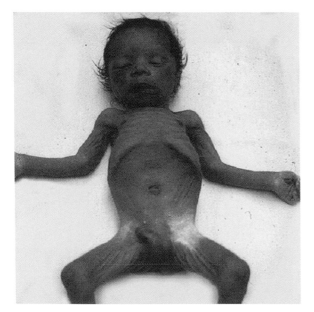

FIGURE 14.38 This child died of both malnutrition and dehydration. Vitreous humor testing for sodium concentration revealed a sodium of 175. A value over 155 suggests dehydration.

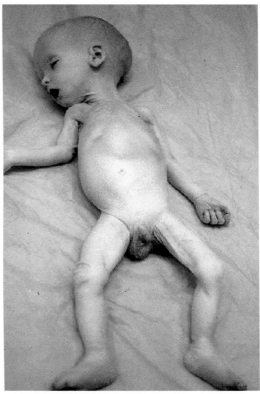

FIGURE 14.39 This baby died of malnutrition. There were no other physical or toxicological abnormalities to otherwise account for death. See next photo.

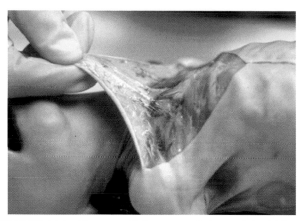

FIGURE 14.40 There was little or no soft tissue (fat) which the child should normally have at this age. The question of dehydration should be answered by determining the sodium concentration in the vitreous humor.

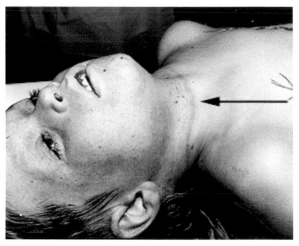

FIGURE 14.41 The thin mark around this child was caused by a window shade cord. He accidentally hanged himself. Notice the red discoloration of the face and neck above the cord mark and not below it.

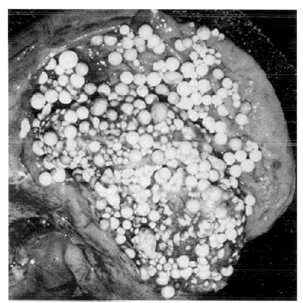

FIGURE 14.42 The inside of this stomach contains hundreds of styrofoam balls. These were swallowed when the child crawled inside a bean bag that he unzipped. He also aspirated many of the balls, causing him to asphyxiate.

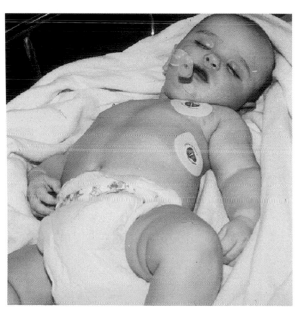

FIGURE 14.43 Sudden Infant Death Syndrome (SIDS) occurs in children under the age of one year. Both the autopsy and the scene investigation must be negative to make this diagnosis.

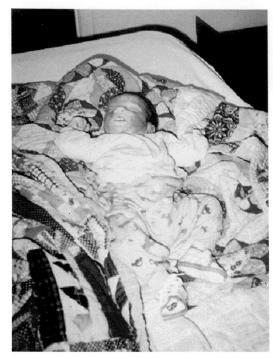

FIGURE 14.44 A SIDS death occurs commonly in a crib. The investigator must make sure there are no pillows or blankets in the sleeping area that could cause suffocation. See next photo.

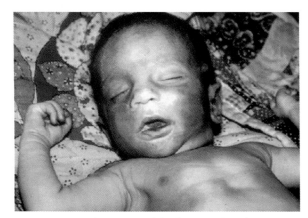

FIGURE 14.47 A closer view of the face reveals pale areas caused by the body lying face down on the bedding. This child may have died of suffocation due to rebreathing the exhaled carbon dioxide.

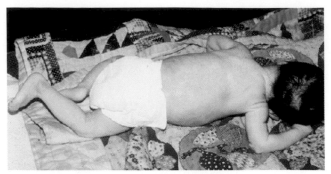

FIGURE 14.45 There is no lividity on the posterior of the body. See next photo.

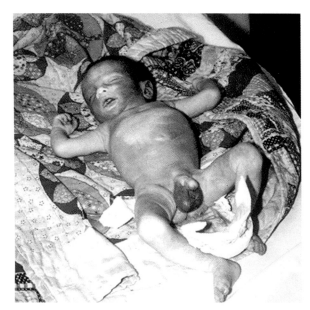

FIGURE 14.46 The livor mortis is prominent on the front of the body. See next photo.

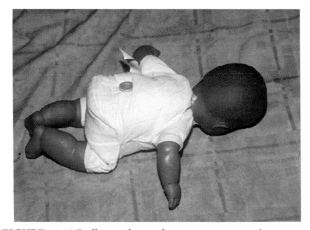

FIGURE 14.48 Dolls may be used to recreate scenes since many infants are removed from the place of death prior to the arrival of law enforcement, paramedics, and death investigators.

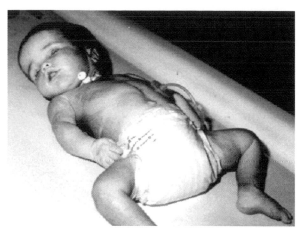

FIGURE 14.49 This child was kept alive by a respirator and lived in a hospital for six weeks after it was shaken. See next photo.

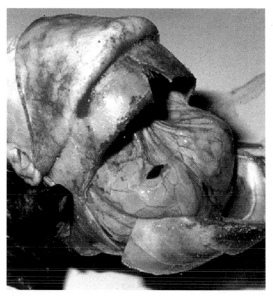

FIGURE 14.50 The brain appears to be flattened and filled with fluid. See next photo.

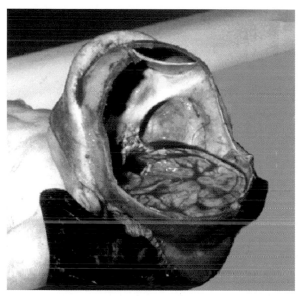

FIGURE 14.51 After weeks in the hospital, the brain became a bag of fluid which collapsed after it was cut. There was little to gain from examining the brain at this stage. The most important time to gain information in this case was at the time of hospitalization. The investigation was more important than the autopsy in this case.

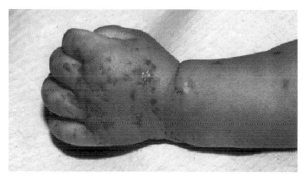

FIGURE 14.52 The marks on this child's arm were caused by roaches after death (anthropophagia).

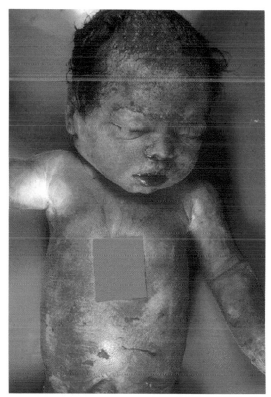

FIGURE 14.53 This baby was discarded in a trash container after birth. The ruling of alive birth versus stillborn must be determined. X-rays are necessary to determine if the baby breathed and swallowed air after birth.

Chapter 15

PEDIATRIC PATHOLOGY CASES

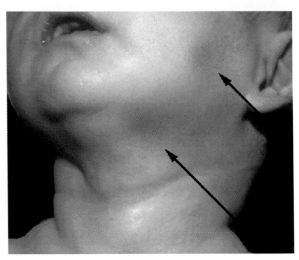

FIGURE 15.1 This six-month-old was brought to the ER dead. He had two bruises on the face. The parent gave a story of finding the child dead. The physician was suspicious because of injuries, such as these contusions. See next photo.

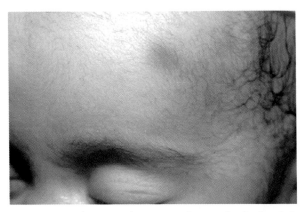

FIGURE 15.2 There was also a contusion on the forehead. See next photo.

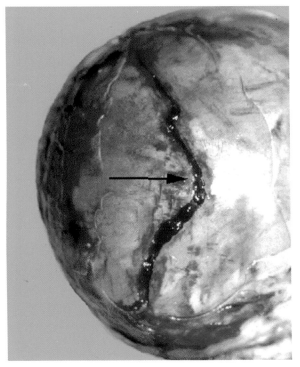

FIGURE 15.3 Autopsy revealed a fracture of the skull which was not picked up on X-ray in the ER. See next photo.

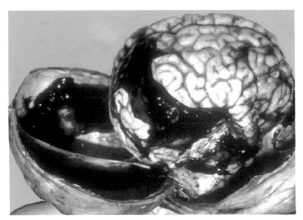

FIGURE 15.4 There were subarachnoid and subdural hemorrhages. See next photo.

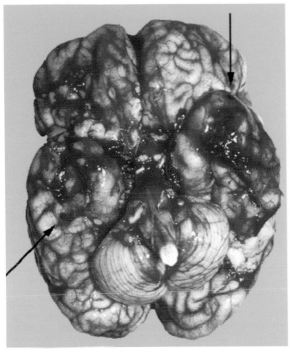

FIGURE 15.5 Although brain contusions are uncommon in this age group, there were numerous ones on this child's brain. See next photo.

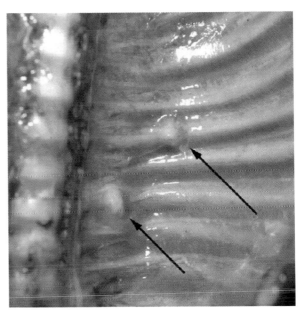

FIGURE 15.6 Healing rib fractures were apparent. This child was abused more than once. He died of blunt trauma to the head.

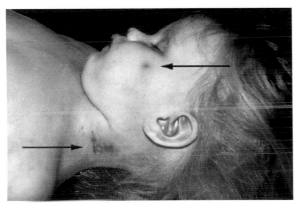

FIGURE 15.7 This child reportedly fell off a chair on which she was standing while eating her supper. Her father said she struck her head on a credenza and then the floor. There were recent contusions and abrasions of the head and neck. See next photo.

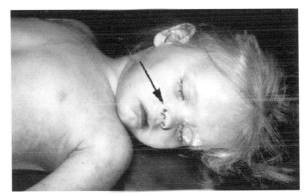

FIGURE 15.8 There was an abrasion on the side of her nose caused by resuscitation attempt. An old yellow contusion on the forehead was barely noticeable at autopsy. See next photo.

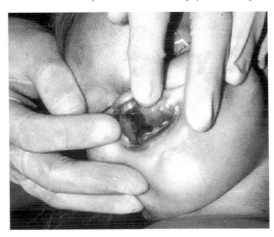

FIGURE 15.9 She had a healing laceration of the upper lip and gum. See next photo.

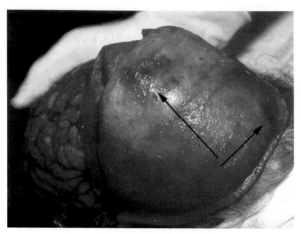

FIGURE 15.10 Two subscalpular hemorrhages had no corresponding external injuries. See next photo.

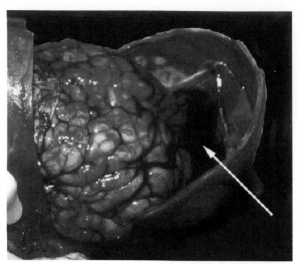

FIGURE 15.11 There was a thin film of subdural hemorrhage and there were retinal hemorrhages. She had been shaken and beaten. She did not receive her injuries as reported by the caretaker.

FIGURE 15.12 The police were called to this yard because a dog was seen playing with a toy which looked like a baby. See next photo.

FIGURE 15.13 The toy was indeed a newborn. See next photo.

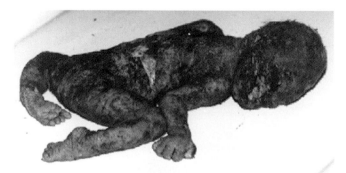

FIGURE 15.14 Injuries were noted; however, their extent could not be determined until the infant was cleaned. See next photo.

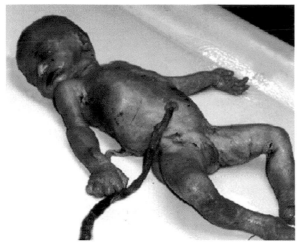

FIGURE 15.15 The baby, with umbilical cord still attached, looked much different when cleaned. See next photo.

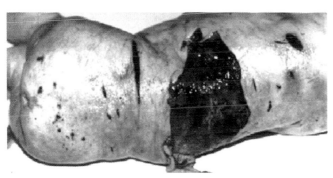

FIGURE 15.17 The large defect extending across the back was caused by the dog. The other cut marks can also be seen. See next photo.

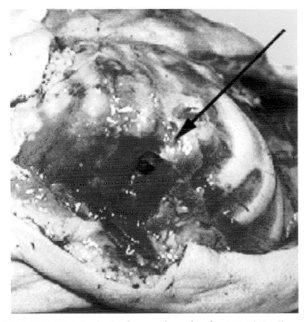

FIGURE 15.19 An incised wound on the chest was initially thought to be a stab wound, but the external chest wall revealed no cutting injury over this wound. See next photo.

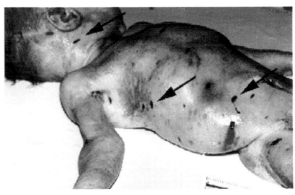

FIGURE 15.16 There were numerous small (less than one inch in length) superficial cut marks over the entire body. See next photo.

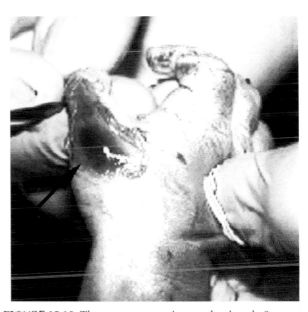

FIGURE 15.18 There was a contusion on the thumb. See next photo.

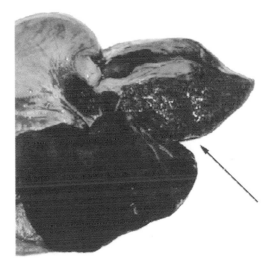

FIGURE 15.20 There was a laceration of the liver (arrow). See next photo.

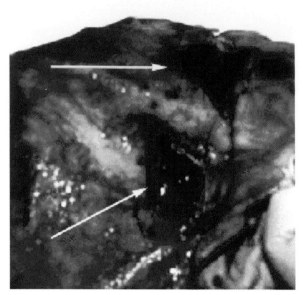

FIGURE 15.21 Two areas of subscalpular hemorrhage were evident. See next photo.

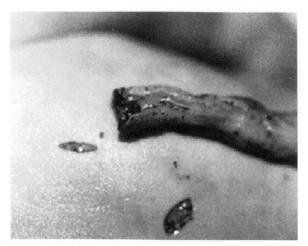

FIGURE 15.22 The umbilical cord had been cut. Two incised wounds can also be seen. The 17-year-old mother admitted having the baby over the toilet in the bathroom of her house. She thought the baby moved briefly. The boyfriend placed the baby in a bag and dropped it over a barbed-wire fence. The cut wounds were from barbed wire and thorns on nearby bushes. The mother and boyfriend were convicted of killing the baby.

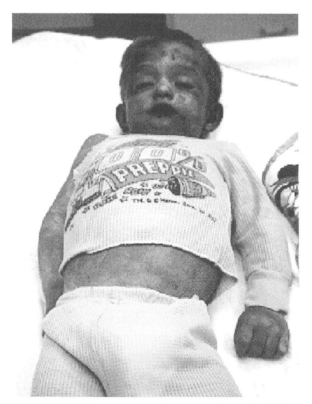

FIGURE 15.23 This two-year-old was brought to the ER in a moribund state. He lived for only a few hours. Neither the mother nor her boyfriend could explain his injuries or death. The child had abdominal surgery nine weeks prior to death. The surgeon was suspicious of abuse at that time because there was a contusion on his arm and some of his head hair appeared to have been pulled out. See next photo.

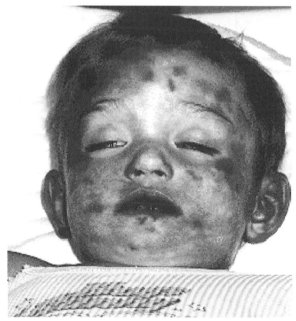

FIGURE 15.24 There were numerous superficial abrasions of the face which looked like rug burns. The lips are dried. X-rays revealed healing fractures of a posterior rib and a clavicle. See next photo.

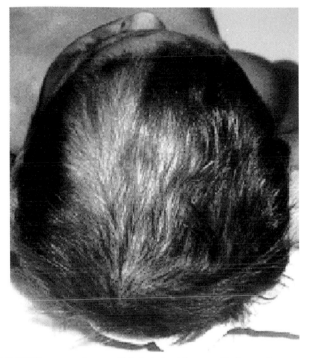

FIGURE 15.25 Some of his hair had been pulled out. See next photo.

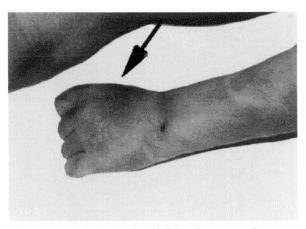

FIGURE 15.26 The back of the left hand was recently contused. See next photo.

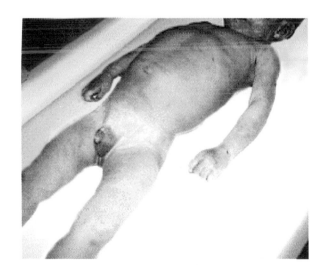

FIGURE 15.28 His abdomen was markedly protruberant. See next photo.

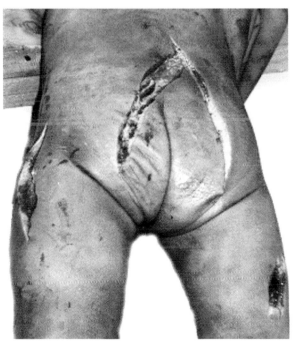

FIGURE 15.27 There were focal soft tissue hemorrhages of the buttocks, lower back, and upper legs from blunt trauma. See next photo.

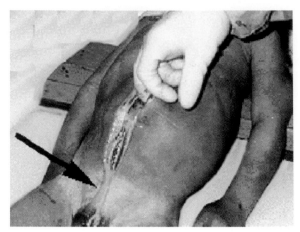

FIGURE 15.29 Pink tan fluid exuded from the peritoneal cavity (arrow) when the abdomen was opened. This fluid, called chylous ascites, was present at the surgery weeks before. See next photo.

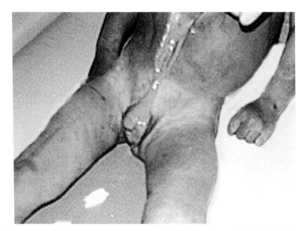

FIGURE 15.30 There was at least 3/4 of a liter of fluid in his belly. See next photo.

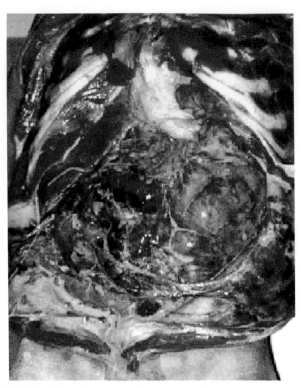

FIGURE 15.31 There was fibrin over all the internal abdominal structures and organs, suggesting peritonitis. The small bowel was completely ruptured near the site of the previous surgery. The final ruling was he died from a blow to the abdomen resulting in a rupture of the small bowel with complicating infection.